Hope Beyond Hope

Copyright © by Bill Mallory 2022

Unless otherwise noted, all Scriptures are from the Holy Bible,

New International Version®, ®. Copyright © 1973, 1978, 1984 by

The International Bible Society. Used by permission of Zondervan. All rights reserved.

Scripture references marked KJV are from the King James Version of the Bible.

Read the scripture references in context for a fuller meaning.

For more books by Bill Mallory
https://billmallorybooks.com

contents

Hope Energizes Faith

Hebrews 11:1-2

11:1 Now faith is being sure of what we hope for and certain of what we do not see. 2 This is what the ancients were commended for.

When Jesus and the Father were discussing the earth and the people, they arrived upon a plan. Because Jesus had an absolute fear of the Lord, respect, and reverence for the Father, they formed humanity around this foundation. They knew that love must be the essence of the strategy. The ability to choose must be a foundational truth, or they would just be creating more angels. The choice is to believe and obey or disbelieve and sin.

Faith is the real entity which is the truth and a viable object, and hope is the quality and the energy that makes that faith occur. So, without our hope, the anticipation of the mind and heart involvement, that thing won't happen. We must believe in making it appear real and touchable rather than remain a figment of our imagination. Our belief system has power from God to create and bring it into three dimensions. Hope is therefore the energy cell of our faith in God. Trust is the tangible outcome that physically proves that the faith was legitimate. So, we have been connected to the almighty in our faith and hope department to produce a visible responding action. The opposite is true, without hope is no joy.

Proverbs 13:12

12 Hope deferred makes the heart sick, but a longing fulfilled is a tree of life.

So, you have to have hope to make faith work. Hearing from God energizes your belief system and stabilizes your hope.

Abraham heard the Word of God and believed that he would have a son.

Genesis 15:4-6

4 Then the word of the LORD came to him: "This man will not be your heir, but a son coming from your own body will be your heir." 5 He took him outside and said, "Look up at the heavens and count the stars--if indeed you can count them." Then he said to him, "So shall your offspring be."

6 Abram believed the LORD, and he credited it to him as righteousness.

When He believed, faith took root.

God told Abraham he would have a son by Sarai and changed her name to Sarah.

Genesis 17:15-16

15 God also said to Abraham, "As for Sarai your wife, you are no longer to call her Sarai; her name will be Sarah. 16 I

will bless her and will surely give you a son by her. I will bless her so that she will be the mother of nations; kings of peoples will come from her."

Then God empowered Abe's hope and asked him to be blameless.

Genesis 17:1-2

17:1 When Abram was ninety-nine years old, the LORD appeared to him and said, "I am God Almighty; walk before me and be blameless. 2 I will confirm my covenant between me and you and will greatly increase your numbers."

God confirmed His promise again, impacting Abraham's children's heritage.

Genesis 17:8

8 The whole land of Canaan, where you are now an alien, I will give as an everlasting possession to you and your descendants after you; and I will be their God."

Abraham laughed at the prospect. He felt joy and wonder. "Could it be?"

Genesis 17:15-22

15 God also said to Abraham, "As for Sarai your wife, you are no longer to call her Sarai; her name will be Sarah. 16 I will bless her and will surely give you a son by her. I will bless her so that she will be the mother of nations; kings of peoples will come from her."

17 Abraham fell facedown; he laughed and said to himself, "Will a son be born to a man a hundred years old? Will Sarah bear a child at the age of ninety?" 18 And Abraham said to God, "If only Ishmael might live under your blessing!"

19 Then God said, "Yes, but your wife Sarah will bear you a son, and you will call him Isaac. I will establish my covenant with him as an everlasting covenant for his descendants after him. 20 And as for Ishmael, I have heard you: I will surely bless him; I will make him fruitful and will greatly increase his numbers. He will be the father of twelve rulers, and I will make him into a great nation. 21 But my covenant I will establish with Isaac, whom Sarah will bear to you by this time next year."

Sarah laughed at the thought of hope completed.

Genesis 18:10-15

10 Then the LORD said, "I will surely return to you about this time next year, and Sarah your wife will have a son."

Now Sarah was listening at the entrance to the tent, which was behind him. 11 Abraham and Sarah were already old and well advanced in years, and Sarah was past the age of childbearing. 12 So Sarah laughed to herself as she thought, "After I am worn out and my master is old, will I now have this pleasure?"

13 Then the LORD said to Abraham, "Why did Sarah laugh and say, 'Will I really have a child, now that I am old?' 14 Is anything too hard for the LORD? I will return to you at the appointed time next year and Sarah will have a son."

15 Sarah was afraid, so she lied and said, "I did not laugh."

But he said, "Yes, you did laugh."

Abe's hope was fully matured and he fathered a son. His trust was complete and he named the child Isaac

Genesis 21:1-3

21:1 Now the LORD was gracious to Sarah as he had said, and the LORD did for Sarah what he had promised. 2 Sarah became pregnant and bore a son to Abraham in his old age, at the very time God had promised him. 3 Abraham gave the name Isaac to the son Sarah bore him.

Acts 3:24-26

24 "Indeed, all the prophets from Samuel on, as many as have spoken, have foretold these days. 25 And you are heirs of the prophets and of the covenant God made with your fathers. He said to Abraham, 'Through your offspring all peoples on earth will be blessed.'

Abraham was the father of the patriarchs.

Acts 7:8

8 Then he gave Abraham the covenant of circumcision. And Abraham became the father of Isaac and circumcised him eight days after his birth. Later Isaac became the father of Jacob, and Jacob became the father of the twelve patriarchs.

Hope is powered by the Holy Spirit

Romans 15:13

13 May the God of hope fill you with all joy and peace as you trust in him, so that you may overflow with hope by the power of the Holy Spirit.

Abraham is now the father of the faithful.

Romans 4:11-12

11 And he received the sign of circumcision, a seal of the righteousness that he had by faith while he was still uncircumcised. So then, he is the father of all who believe but have not been circumcised, in order that righteousness might be credited to them. 12 And he is also the father of the circumcised who not only are circumcised but who also

walk in the footsteps of the faith that our father Abraham had before he was circumcised.

God's response to belief is to reward the believer, which is also proof that He hears. God chooses interaction to build a relationship, which is His immediate goal, and why He sent Jesus to the earth. He rates His relationship with us very highly and fulfills His unlimited love for His creation. God is happy to make you happy by empowering your hope through His Holy Spirit.

Hebrews 11:6

 6 And without faith it is impossible to please God, because anyone who comes to him must believe that he exists and that he rewards those who earnestly seek him.

We must engage the fear of the Lord, or faith will not work. Respect and reverence are important in this context. A person could have fear of the Lord believing that if they made Him mad, He could smash them. But add the other qualifier reverence, and fear is changed to an attraction of love which negates evil thoughts. If we do not have respect for God, that is akin to unbelief, so how can you talk to someone you don't believe exists

God is so passionately in love with everybody, that even children are rated highly in God's economy.

Mark 9:42

42 "And if anyone causes one of these little ones who believe in me to sin, it would be better for him to be thrown into the sea with a large millstone tied around his neck.

God has assigned the little children probably two angels to be always with them. These are to protect and guide them and hopefully they can know and receive the Holy Spirit to guide them to Jesus on earth and on into the Kingdom of God. They may be friends in Heaven. Parents are responsible and commissioned to be their teachers and direct them in the things of God and to God.

The parents have a responsibility to train the child in the way he should go.

Ephesians 6:4

4 And, ye fathers, provoke not your children to wrath: but bring them up in the nurture and admonition of the Lord. KJV

The parent's charge is,

Proverbs 22:6

6 Train a child in the way he should go,

and when he is old he will not turn from it.

Then the children can have a history of relationship with the Lord, and how we should think about and pray for our kids and family. You can instill in them hope in the Lord.

This is so important because lots of times we utter five-second prayers that we don't have the time to compile all the right components to make it a proper prayer. Even if we just blurt it out as the thought comes through our mind and back to what we were thinking about, God hears it. Our faith must include past five-second prayer answers. We have built trust in God's answers that we no longer doubt, but expect a positive answer with a righteous statement that He is listening and giving us what we want.

When my wife takes her car on the road, I pray for her protection and then go on with what I am doing, trusting that He is taking care of her. And He does.

When I start a job at work I pray for the fear of the Lord, wisdom, knowledge, understanding and other things I can think of that applies to the job. I know he answers so I confidently go to work. I can tell He responds because my mind lines up with what I need.

Mark 11:24

24 Therefore I tell you, whatever you ask for in prayer, believe that you have received it, and it will be yours.

Believe Jesus for whom He said He is.

John 3:17-18

17 For God did not send his Son into the world to condemn the world, but to save the world through him. 18 Whoever believes in him is not condemned, but whoever does not believe stands condemned already because he has not believed in the name of God's one and only Son.

Prayer works. That is why I rely on it daily.

Mark 11:22-24

22 "Have faith in God," Jesus answered. 23 "I tell you the truth, if anyone says to this mountain, 'Go, throw yourself into the sea,' and does not doubt in his heart but believes that what he says will happen, it will be done for him. 24 Therefore I tell you, whatever you ask for in prayer, believe that you have received it, and it will be yours.

I want to put you first in everything I think, do, and say today.

When your spirit is hooked up to the Holy Spirit – you are tapped into the power of God. You have the insight of the Lord and can process the ideas of God.

Respect God's presence knowing He is responding.

Zechariah 4:6

6 So he said to me, "This is the word of the LORD to Zerubbabel: 'Not by might nor by power, but by my Spirit,' says the LORD Almighty.

When speaking in tongues, the Lord can teach the things of the Spirit of God by osmosis, to your spirit. The Holy Spirit speaks through your spirit which is next to your soul and can learn from the dialog. In tongues will gain wisdom, knowledge, and understanding of the mind of Christ in you.

Joshua and Caleb could go into the Promised Land because they believed in God, and Joshua loved the presence of the Lord. They hoped to go into the Promised Land for forty years. And finally, their trust brought them in.

They had faith in God's word.

Hope is what gave them the spiritual power to continue in faith in God's word

Jerimiah, Isaiah, and Bible writers believed in the Holy Spirit and it happened years later.

John saw the Angel of God and wrote Revelation. God's Spirit brought His Word to the writers of the Bible. God spoke all of it.

2 Timothy 3:15-17

15 and how from infancy you have known the holy Scriptures, which are able to make you wise for salvation through faith in Christ Jesus. 16 All Scripture is God-breathed and is useful for teaching, rebuking, correcting and training in righteousness, 17 so that the man of God may be thoroughly equipped for every good work.

We can trust the Bible because we trust God.

POINTS OF INTEREST

1. How much faith do you put in the Bible as the Word of God?

2. Explain the progression of faith, hope, and trust.

3. How do you train a child in the way he should go?

WORD OF WISDOM

Abraham was known as the father of the faithful. God brought them out to bring them in.

Deuteronomy 7:5-9

6 For you are a people holy to the LORD your God. The LORD your God has chosen you out of all the peoples on the face of the earth to be his people, his treasured possession.

7 The LORD did not set his affection on you and choose you because you were more numerous than other peoples, for you were the fewest of all peoples. 8 But it was because the LORD loved you and kept the oath he swore to your forefathers that he brought you out with a mighty hand and redeemed you from the land of slavery, from the power of Pharaoh king of Egypt. 9 Know therefore that the LORD your God is God; he is the faithful God, keeping his covenant of love to a thousand generations of those who love him and keep his commands.

My hope story

As I was praying in the temporary church building, we rented in 1983, a plan began to develop. This an old abandoned school building that we could rent until we could formulate the next step for expansion.

The school grounds included a field with a running track oval which would be a good place for an outreach building. It had been neglected for so long that the wooden floor was badly warped from leaking water. I would walk the halls and pray with nobody else there. Then the vision converted into my being involved in missions.

The problem was that I could not see myself being a missionary with my set of skills.

We lost some members and we could not pay the rent because the people that were renting our old church building couldn't pay their rent so we moved back into our old church building. But I did gain Roberta for my wife and we were married in the old school building's gymnasium. That was a good gain out of that church move.

Sometime after that, I went to Mexico and helped build a church building. I arrived the day after the sewer blew up from waste gasoline that had been dumped into the sewer to get rid of it. A mile-long stretch of suburb street was a bomb from the gasses trapped in the pipe, then ignited. Many fragile built houses crumbled and many people died. My job in the new church was to mix cement and carry it up the stairs. We completed the roof before the monsoon season started.

Next, I went with the pastor to the Philippines Islands to preach at their graduation celebration from Bible school. He preached and I carried the stuff.

Next, I and my wife went to Copper Island, Vancouver Island to help missionaries with a native youth camp. I built a hot water shower from a cold waterfall. We built a water heater out of an old fuel cell with water pipe coils in it to heat the water collected from the waterfall. Then I found out that I also had to chop the wood for the fire. It ran well for about 40 kids to get a shower when the tide was out.

The shower consisted of a stall on a platform with a pipe and shower head and plastic around for privacy. To get hot water, you would turn the water flow down to give the gravity flow water time to heat in the coils, and turn the flow up to cool it by putting more cold water into the spray. It worked just fine. I had seen the plans in the Mechanics Illustrated magazine a few months before we went to the island.

Next, I was invited to help work on a mission building for the children in Uganda but I had to stop in Nairobi, Kenya because the dictator closed Entebbe airport in Uganda. In Nairobi, I helped a missionary with her house repair and prayed along with her at the Women's Aglow meeting.

The next adjustment was that I would get other people to go out and do missionary work.

After each trip, I would ask myself and God, "Am I a goer, or a sender?" The answer would always come back that God wants me to be involved in sending and not going to the mission field.

I did not see myself in that profession doing anything helpful on the mission field either, but the dream persisted. The next addition to the vision from the Lord was in the form of a directive to me.

The Lord said to me, "I want you to train, send out, and support a thousand teams of missionaries." I accepted the dictate, when He said in the next prayer session, "Because the other person I was choosing turned me down, I give to you his thousand also to send out. That put more meat on the bone for me. I'm still working out the details remaining of the mystery, but I did not doubt God for this 3 years.

One day I mentioned this dream to a friend of mine and he invited me to a restaurant with him and a relative of his. He said, Bill, I want you to repeat this dream of yours to him. So, I told him again that the Lord wants me to train up, send out and support 2000 teams of missionaries. They confirmed together that this was not possible. "You can't do this." This effort to discourage me from vision, only bolstered my faith and hope in the Lord to do it. I said, "I know I can't, but the Lord can." This answer boiled up from my heart like a volcano and still carries the same weight as the first. We all left the restaurant the same as we came in, except I was more fired up and confident. This is still my position.

The question persisted on just how I could do this monumental job, I'm just a machinist. This unshakeable directive would not leave my heart. I wrote it down and prayed about it a lot and it remains.

In the meanwhile, I was working at Boeing on an important job and they wanted me to work every day for some months. Even a non-Christian asked me how could I, being a Christian, work on Sundays. I should have taken the warning seriously, but just passed it off.

Unbeknownst to me, there were polyps forming in my colon and becoming cancerous. After a time, I became exhausted and couldn't work, so I had to go to the hospital, which I don't really care much for, but I had never been debilitated like that before.

The doctor examined me and found a cancerous polyp in my colon and came to me and told me, Bill, you have cancer. My nonchalant response surprised me, but I was not worried. You are supposed to be all depressed when you hear that 'C' word. How come did I respond to the bad news that way?

My wife prayed for me, the pastor, and the congregation prayed and two days later the doctor took out the polyp and examined it, and found no cancer. When he told me, I was glad God healed me in two days, but not too exuberantly because I still had three weeks to recuperate.

Finally, I remembered that two of my friends were healed from cancer in the past year. So, my faith kicked in and I had instant faith for healing. In two days, the healing turned into a miracle. The witness of my friends had power in my spirit. That bad news was short-cut into a miracle, and now everybody hears about it. It is too good to keep to myself.

I had time to think about all the happenings while on a three-week regroup in bed from exhaustion. So, I started writing. I wrote a booklet on healing. God can heal a person from the plague of HIV disease. After that, I started writing a book on what was happening at our old church. It included the evils and divisive ways of the devil. It expanded to 61 chapters about spiritual warfare, "One A Day Spiritual Warfare", and then I published it.

In my following prayer time, the subject of my calling came up. I began to envision that my writing could be used to make money for supporting missions. I believe I heard the Lord tell me that He wanted me to write 100 books for the soon-coming revival. So, after writing and publishing two more books, I reasoned that I could not do this. Publishing costs thousands of dollars, each, so I went into wonderment mode. While I was treading water in my mind,

I learned about inexpensive publishing on amazon. This set me back a couple of years in my supposed schedule, but I have run out of options.

Relying on the Lord to reinvigorate the hope of my dream. He gave me the knowledge and ability to write books and get them published affordably.

Now I go back to the Lord for increased hope to carry through with the vision. I have written and published nineteen books in ten years, and the math has me coming up short of my 100-book schedule. This drives me back to the 'hope bank' for more power from the Holy Spirit.

Romans 15:13

13 May the God of hope fill you with all joy and peace as you trust in him, so that you may overflow with hope by the power of the Holy Spirit.

Don't worry, we have time, I'm only 85 years old and just past mid-life.

I know my hope in the Holy Spirit will bolster my hope in His calling to get the job done. He will help me to trust in Him sufficiently.

POINTS OF INTEREST

1. Has God put something on your heart that needs extra hope?
2. Explain the power of the Holy Spirit to strengthen hope.
3. Since the Holy Spirit is God's spirit, is there anything He cannot do?
4. Do you have a lingering hope story that only the Holy Spirit can bring to pass?

WORD OF WISDOM

I am honored to be given this task to write your principles for the people that come behind me to learn them. I feel similar to David in my qualifications and what you have done for me.

1 Chronicles 29:14-17

14 "But who am I, and who are my people, that we should be able to give as generously as this? Everything comes from you, and we have given you only what comes from your hand. 15 We are aliens and strangers in your sight, as were all our forefathers. Our days on earth are like a shadow, without hope. 16 O LORD our God, as for all this abundance that we have provided for building you a temple for your Holy Name, it comes from your hand, and all of it belongs to you. 17 I know, my God, that you test the heart and are pleased with integrity. All these things have I given willingly and with honest intent. And now I have seen with joy how willingly your people who are here have given to you.

And I need His constant help to be able to maneuver this complicated world. Thank you, Lord. The fear of the Lord in my driver.

The Love of God

The Love of God is the realm that gives life.

Before the creation of Earth, there was no time, clock, or calendar because these calculations belong to the rotation of the earth. God lives in a timeless eternity with His Son and His Spirit. They were always and forever existent.

I visualize eternity as a large gold ball with a small square scratched on it for the earth.

1 John 4:13-18

13 We know that we live in him and he in us, because he has given us of his Spirit. 14 And we have seen and testify that the Father has sent his Son to be the Savior of the world. 15 If anyone acknowledges that Jesus is the Son of God, God lives in him and he in God. 16 And so we know and rely on the love God has for us.

God is love. Whoever lives in love lives in God, and God in him. 17 In this way, love is made complete among us so that we will have confidence on the day of judgment, because in this world we are like him. 18 There is no fear in love. But perfect love drives out fear, because fear has to do with punishment. The one who fears is not made perfect in love.

This fear is a 'terror' fear, not the fear of the Lord, meaning respect, and reverence which is total love.

Love one another

1 John 4:7-12

7 Dear friends, let us love one another, for love comes from God. Everyone who loves has been born of God and knows God. 8 Whoever does not love does not know God, because

God is love. 9 This is how God showed his love among us: He sent his one and only Son into the world that we might live through him. 10 This is love: not that we loved God, but that he loved us and sent his Son as an atoning sacrifice for our sins. 11 Dear friends, since God so loved us, we also ought to love one another. 12 No one has ever seen God; but if we love one another, God lives in us and his love is made complete in us.

This should be our attitude toward God, to love what He loves.

Matthew 22:37-40

37 Jesus replied: "'Love the Lord your God with all your heart and with all your soul and with all your mind.' 38 This is the first and greatest commandment. 39 And the second is like it: 'Love your neighbor as yourself.' 40 All the Law and the Prophets hang on these two commandments."

The fear of the Lord means to have respect and reverence for God. Nothing eternally good happens to humans unless we have respect and reverence for God.

Proverbs 9:10

10 "The fear of the LORD is the beginning of wisdom,

and knowledge of the Holy one is understanding.

The Holy One is Jesus.

All God made is good. I like to say in response to a 'have a good day greeting, "I know it's a good day because God made it."

Genesis 1:1-5

1:1 In the beginning God created the heavens and the earth. 2 Now the earth was formless and empty, darkness was over the surface of the deep, and the Spirit of God was hovering over the waters.

3 And God said, "Let there be light," and there was light. 4 God saw that the light was good, and he separated the light from the darkness. 5 God called the light "day," and the darkness he called "night." And there was evening, and there was morning--the first day.

That was a good day.

Genesis 1:25

And God saw that it was good.

I respect God because He made all creation by His word. That could also mean He made it by Jesus and Jesus is also called the Word of God. Jesus had a firm integral fear of the Lord.

I count it an extreme pleasure and honor to be individually made by God, the Creator of everything. He perfectly made me and put on me His 'signature', which is a part of Himself, in me to give Him glory and gave me His personal autograph as a claim to my uniqueness, as He does for everybody. It is like a notable painter's distinctive style of painting. No clones or duplicates in His production line. God intentionally creates babies uniquely, time, and place for specific parents to perfectly fit into His purpose in the Kingdom of God. And He starts their heart pumping 18 days after conception.

The brilliant growth process of teaching cells what to do and where to grow and multiply. It is a TLC miracle. A newly conceived baby's heart starts to be a working blood pump in about 18 days. Every time I see that sign, I worship God.

This Awesome Creator made everything with precision and care. Even the elements that make up the air are of the correct proportion. The oxygen and nitrogen percentages are perfect for supporting both and stabilizing air to breathe and fire to burn. Tricky balance. God made the moon swing around the earth at the precise speed to stay in a certain orbit and not crash into the earth nor be flung away into space on a tangent, never to be seen again. The attraction of the moon on the ocean causes the tide to ebb and flow which washes and scrubs the sandy shore. And the Earth tips 45 degrees, north, and south every year to define the seasons. Smart God.

God tells of His awesome Love. Thank you, Lord Jesus.

Romans 8:37-39

37 No, in all these things we are more than conquerors through him who loved us. 38 For I am convinced that neither death nor life, neither angels nor demons, neither the present nor the future, nor any powers, 39 neither height nor depth, nor anything else in all creation, will be able to separate us from the love of God that is in Christ Jesus our Lord.

We are secure in His Love.

With credentials as powerful as this, who could deny His security?

2 Timothy 1:8-12

8 So do not be ashamed to testify about our Lord, or ashamed of me his prisoner. But join with me in suffering for the gospel, by the power of God, 9 who has saved us and called us to a holy life-not because of anything we have done but because of his own purpose and grace. This grace was given us in Christ Jesus before the beginning of time, 10 but it has now been revealed through the appearing of

our Savior, Christ Jesus, who has destroyed death and has brought life and immortality to light through the gospel. 11 And of this gospel I was appointed a herald and an apostle and a teacher. 12 That is why I am suffering as I am. Yet I am not ashamed, because I know whom I have believed, and am convinced that he is able to guard what I have entrusted to him for that day.

God has fierce angels on duty.

Plus, He knows what we need. So, make your focus on the Kingdom of God.

Luke 12:28-31

29 And do not set your heart on what you will eat or drink; do not worry about it. 30 For the pagan world runs after all such things, and your Fath1er knows that you need them. 31 But seek his kingdom, and these things will be given to you as well.

God is so consistent that I can have total faith in Him and His attributes and depend on His love.

POINTS OF INTEREST
1. What do you love about God?

2. Do you feel secure in what you have given God?

3. What have you given Him for safe keeping?

WORD OF WISDOM

We have come a long way to be saved, but thanks to Jesus for making the way.

Titus 3:3-8

3 At one time we too were foolish, disobedient, deceived and enslaved by all kinds of passions and pleasures. We lived in malice and envy, being hated and hating one another. 4 But when the kindness and love of God our Savior appeared, 5 he saved us, not because of righteous things we had done, but because of his mercy. He saved us through the washing of rebirth and renewal by the Holy Spirit, 6 whom he poured out on us generously through Jesus Christ our Savior, 7 so that, having been justified by his grace, we might become heirs having the hope of eternal life. 8 This is a trustworthy saying. And I want you to stress these things, so that those who have trusted in God may be careful to devote themselves to doing what is good. These things are excellent and profitable for everyone.

Faith

Those who are righteous, live by faith. This is the lifestyle of those who love Jesus. But, faith in what?

Romans 1:16-17

16 I am not ashamed of the gospel, because it is the power of God for the salvation of everyone who believes: first for the Jew, then for the Gentile. 17 For in the gospel a righteousness from God is revealed, a righteousness that is by faith from first to last, just as it is written: "The righteous will live by faith."

Faith is deeper than physical eyesight, it has to do with our spirit.

Hebrews 11:1-2

11:1 Now faith is being sure of what we hope for and certain of what we do not see.

When we have faith, we can know it will happen. Then when hope kicks in there is the power to prepare for action. Then when we have trust, confidence transfers to the ability to do it.

When our faith system is governing our life, our whole being is regulated by the fact of the Gospel. Saved by Jesus is our Lord He forgave our sins and we now have a home in Heaven. We have no worries or worldly concerns that could take us away from our love of God. Augmented by the power in the Hope of the Holy Spirit we have a shield against unseen enemies. We have trust in the protection of our assigned angels from bodily harm and the knowledge that God supplies all our needs, there is nothing left to dilute our faith.

In the Jewish wedding, there is faith in marriage and the process is discussed. Hope starts the preparation for the wedding and adds substance to the wedding. Then when it is all ready to start, the father has to say it is time to go. This is the power to make it happen and the trust is in the completion of the marriage.

We, therefore, have received a communication beyond the natural and lives in our 'heart', which is that which connects with the Holy Spirit of God. God is making a connection with His creation. It is like a spiritual 'umbilical' cord that brings life to an unborn baby.

Enoch had this connection with God that God wanted to use him as an example of a righteous person who pleased God and believed in God without using his eyes. He was one that God was eager to reward with the peace of Heaven bypassing the difficulties of earth.

Hebrews 11:5-6

5 By faith Enoch was taken from this life, so that he did not experience death; he could not be found, because God had taken him away. For before he was taken, he was commended as one who pleased God. 6 And without faith it is impossible to please God, because anyone who comes to him must believe that he exists and that he rewards those who earnestly seek him.

There is this little 'faith box' down there to collect faith things for future reference. This box lies between my soul and spirit to receive from the Holy Spirit. I put in there miracles, answers to prayers, verses in the Bible, the truth that I read, and God things that I see and hear. Truth is the filter I keep activated by revisiting the Bible, supplied with new truths and ready to meet new spiritual challenges that come up in life. I keep this filter turned on when I listen to people advocating some ideas that I question. I want to keep the truth in my spirit pure so wrong ideas won't taint my heart.

My conscience is my messenger that runs back and forth to take the training of my spirit from the Holy Spirit to check if my soul got it and correct it if it did not. It will send a message back if it does not line with the truth, and for the soul to take corrective action, or be bothered about it. The conscience hates discord and opposition between our soul and spirit. They need to be the same and synchronized. Dissidence is displeasing. Righteousness cannot handle this. This corrective action keeps the consciences clean.

I read the Bible daily to keep it fresh and relevant. It goes into its own storage area of the 'box' that is instantly accessed, quicker than a digital hard drive. I use this coordinator constantly as my Bible filter when I read anything or listen to anybody, to compare it with the truth. The truth division is adjacent to the faith box for instant access.

Once in a Bible study, this man said, "God helps those who help themselves." And instantly I shouted, "That is not true. That's from the pit of Hell." From my Bible reading, this thought rang false, and I later found where it was in the Bible. God helps those who believe in Him.

Romans 8:37-39

37 No, in all these things we are more than conquerors through him who loved us. 38 For I am convinced that neither death nor life, neither angels nor demons, neither the present nor the future, nor any powers, 39 neither height nor depth, nor anything else in all creation, will be able to separate us from the love of God that is in Christ Jesus our Lord.

Believers of old were burnt at the stake if they would not renounce Jesus. Hope in Jesus strengthened their faith.

POINTS OF INTEREST

1. Do you believe faith needs to be based upon the truth?

2. Where does faith come from?

3. Do you believe everybody has a little faith?

WORD OF WISDOM

We are all created with enough faith to get saved. But, then what do you do with it?

Hebrews 10:38

38 But my righteous one will live by faith. And if he shrinks back, I will not be pleased with him."

Without faith, one could believe that the universe could have made itself.

Hebrews 11:33

By faith we understand that the universe was formed at God's command, so that what is seen was not made out of what was visible.

The power of Hope

Hope then is the power that empowers and sustains faith and develops belief and trust. Hope is the door to the dream room. Hope is the power of the Spirit that we use to authenticate the idea to continue in our belief.

We need to put hope in context with faith because hope is what makes faith work.

Hebrews 11:1-2

11:1 Now faith is being sure of what we hope for and certain of what we do not see.

If we don't hope for it, we can then doubt it will happen. There needs to be some anticipation and expectation, for our desired result to activate God's hand. Hope protects against doubt and keeps it at arm's length.

Jesus is our Hope.

Jerimiah 17:12-13

12 A glorious throne, exalted from the beginning,

is the place of our sanctuary.

13 O LORD, the hope of Israel,

all who forsake you will be put to shame.

Those who turn away from you will be written in the dust

because they have forsaken the LORD,

the spring of living water.

He is our hope because He said He is the life and the way to the Father.

So, with respect to God, we must put Jesus and His Word as the highest priority in our life. Learn all you can about Jesus, know it, and do it. Press into Him.

John 14:6-7

6 Jesus answered, "I am the way and the truth and the life. No one comes to the Father except through me. 7 If you really knew me, you would know my Father as well. From now on, you do know him and have seen him."

Hope in Jesus will never be put to shame.

Psalms 25:1-3

To you, O LORD, I lift up my soul; 2 in you I trust, O my God. Do not let me be put to shame, nor let my enemies triumph over me. 3 No one whose hope is in you will ever be put to shame,

I seldom weaken, but then I come back to hope in Jesus, and He is immediately available for conversation and companionship by the ever-present Holy Spirit.

Without hope, we have little power. It is depleted.

Proverbs 13:12

12 Hope deferred makes the heart sick,

but a longing fulfilled is a tree of life.

But when hope returns, power for trust returns.

The Father is the God of hope, which is a lot of power.

Romans 15:13

13 Now the God of hope fill you with all joy and peace in believing, that ye may abound in hope, through the power of the Holy Ghost. KJV

Our trust in Him through hope is fruitful with peace and Joy.

We hope in Jesus.

1 Thessalonians 1:3

3 Remembering without ceasing your work of faith, and labour of love, and patience of hope in our Lord Jesus Christ, in the sight of God and our Father; KJV

Extend your love for God to those outside the Kingdom of God so they can have hope in Jesus Christ by offering them the love of the Gospel and including them in your friendship. Pray for them and invite them to Jesus and to His church.

Ephesians 2:11-13

11 Therefore, remember that formerly you who are Gentiles by birth and called "uncircumcised" by those who call themselves "the circumcision" (that done in the body by the hands of men)- 12 remember that at that time you were separate from Christ, excluded from citizenship in Israel and foreigners to the covenants of the promise, without hope and without God in the world. 13 But now in Christ Jesus you who once were far away have been brought near through the blood of Christ.

Because of our accepting the blood of Jesus we have powerful hope for life.

When the energy leaks out of hope, the faith is exhausted.

Ezekiel 19:5

5 "'When she saw her hope unfulfilled,

her expectation gone,
Hope is dynamic.

POINTS OF INTEREST

1. Who is first in your life?

2. What is first in your life faith, hope, or trust?

3. Explain hope.

WORD OF WISDOM

Jesus is our hope.

1 Timothy 1:1

1:1 Paul, an apostle of Christ Jesus by the command of God our Savior and of Christ Jesus our hope,

We have hope through the presence of Jesus and his teaching us the Bible in this life.

Romans 15:4

4 For everything that was written in the past was written to teach us, so that through endurance and the encouragement of the Scriptures we might have hope.

The Father is the God of hope.

Hope will remain on into Heaven.

1 Corinthians 13:12-13

12 Now we see but a poor reflection as in a mirror; then we shall see face to face. Now I know in part; then I shall know fully, even as I am fully known.

13 And now these three remain: faith, hope and love. But the greatest of these is love.

All God's children are called to our hope Jesus as a unit.

Ephesians 4:2-6

3 Make every effort to keep the unity of the Spirit through the bond of peace. 4 There is one body and one Spirit- just as you were called to one hope when you were called- 5 one Lord, one faith, one baptism; 6 one God and Father of all, who is over all and through all and in all.

Faith and Love spring up from hope.

Colossians 1:4-6

5 the faith and love that spring from the hope that is stored up for you in heaven and that you have already heard about in the word of truth, the gospel 6 that has come to you.

Jesus Christ is our hope of glory.

Colossians 1:26-27

27 To them God has chosen to make known among the Gentiles the glorious riches of this mystery, which is Christ in you, the hope of glory.

Jesus is our hope of salvation.

1 Thessalonians 5:7-10

8 But since we belong to the day, let us be self-controlled, putting on faith and love as a breastplate, and the hope of salvation as a helmet. 9 For God did not appoint us to

suffer wrath but to receive salvation through our Lord Jesus Christ.

My grandmother gave me that anchor in Jesus long ago.

We have a living hope because Jesus rose from the dead.

1 Peter 1:3-5

3 Praise be to the God and Father of our Lord Jesus Christ! In his great mercy he has given us new birth into a living hope through the resurrection of Jesus Christ from the dead, 4 and into an inheritance that can never perish, spoil or fade-kept in heaven for you

Hope in the Lord.

Isaiah 40:30-31

30 Even youths grow tired and weary, and young men stumble and fall;

31 but those who hope in the LORD will renew their strength. They will soar on wings like eagles; they will run and not grow weary, they will walk and not be faint.

The Spirit of God is the power for hope, peace, and joy.

Romans 15:13

13 May the God of hope fill you with all joy and peace as you trust in him, so that you may overflow with hope by the power of the Holy Spirit.

I can testify that this really works.

Trust

Trust comes out of a storehouse of positive experiences with the Lord. This includes miracles and truths you saw, read, and heard. When you put all of these types of involvements into your 'faith box' and rely upon them to be repeated, your trust level rises to the top. Then you can trust your trust.

We can trust that hope is empowered by the Holy Spirit.

When I was in the hospital the doctor said I had cancer. I expressed that I was not concerned. Later I was surprised that I was so aloof but remembered that two of my friends had been cured of cancer in the past year. That gave me trust that I would be healed also, and I was healed in two days. As I trusted in my knowledge of their miracle I could also be healed. I like miracles.

Trust acts upon the determined validity of the subject expressed in our faith and hope with no doubt. Each of these steps needs a positive response to moving ahead to see the fruit of my faith in word and action.

Keep in mind as you check through the Holy Spirit, the Bible, and the discerned soundness of the Word of God. You need to be confident that this thought is in the right time, place, and venue to either be pondered or expressed.

Continually put the Lord's knowledge before your own.

Proverbs 3:5-6

5 Trust in the LORD with all your heart

and lean not on your own understanding;

6 in all your ways acknowledge him,

and he will make your paths straight.

In the presence of Jesus, all this managing can be worked in an instant to act on or not act on. The Holy Spirit is our competent discretion manager. Always check with Him.

David was assured that by trusting that God would be true to His word, he would be saved from his many enemies. He put his life on the line and did not worry out of control for his safety.

Psalms 20: 6-7

6 Now I know that the LORD saves his anointed;

he answers him from his holy heaven

with the saving power of his right hand.

7 Some trust in chariots and some in horses,

but we trust in the name of the LORD our God.

We can trust and rely upon God to keep His word as we obey it. Whatever God says in the Bible we can depend on to be true when we do the right thing.

So, when the Bible talks about the future that we can't see. We can have confidence that it is reliable so we can live our life accordingly.

We can say with David,

Psalms 26:1-2

Vindicate me, O LORD, for I have led a blameless life; I have trusted in the LORD without wavering. 2 Test me, O LORD, and try me, examine my heart and my mind;

Don't let wavering dilute your trust in the Lord.

James 1:5-8

5 If any of you lacks wisdom, he should ask God, who gives generously to all without finding fault, and it will be given to him. 6 But when he asks, he must believe and not doubt, because he who doubts is like a wave of the sea, blown and tossed by the wind. 7 That man should not think he will receive anything from the Lord; 8 he is a double-minded man, unstable in all he does.

You will find that the Lord is trustworthy.

John 14:1-4

14:1 "Do not let your hearts be troubled. Trust in God; trust also in me. 2 In my Father's house are many rooms; if it were not so, I would have told you. I am going there to prepare a place for you. 3 And if I go and prepare a place for you, I will come back and take you to be with me that you also may be where I am. 4 You know the way to the place where I am going."

We come under the scrutiny and discipline of the Holy Spirit. He will help us to become truer as He is true. We can trust His truth and He will prove it.

The Holy Spirit trains us beyond just teaching us, to know and rely on His wisdom to walk in trust in what He says about the future.

I have wondered why mountains jump into my path that I have to deal with. I find out that the Holy Spirit is preparing me for more difficult situations to learn to overcome in the future. I appreciate His complete training.

As we climb up these mountains, we are strengthened in many ways physically, mentally, and spiritually. When I recognized this fact, I began praying for patience. People thought I was crazy. But I know the result of God's quick answer to that request is because He wants us to have endurance and acceptance to wait on Him and obey His word.

1 Corinthians 4:1-2

4:1 So then, men ought to regard us as servants of Christ and as those entrusted with the secret things of God. 2 Now it is required that those who have been given a trust must prove faithful.

Do you see how a person must rely on the truth of God in what He says and act upon what they believe God to have said? They think that was God and it was a true message from the almighty God for me to obey the instructions accordingly.

Then the proof is in the pudding. Did it turn out like I believe God said and was the outcome correct? When you go through test after test and it results in the same and right answer, you can understand the obedience was correct.

Samuel heard the Lord's voice, obeyed, and proved it to be.

1 Samuel 3:3-5, 8-12

3 The lamp of God had not yet gone out, and Samuel was lying down in the temple of the LORD, where the ark of God was. 4 Then the LORD called Samuel.

Samuel answered, "Here I am." 5 And he ran to Eli and said, "Here I am; you called me."

8 The LORD called Samuel a third time, and Samuel got up and went to Eli and said, "Here I am; you called me."

Then Eli realized that the LORD was calling the boy. 9 So Eli told Samuel, "Go and lie down, and if he calls you, say,

'Speak, LORD, for your servant is listening.'" So Samuel went and lay down in his place. 1

10 The LORD came and stood there, calling as at the other times, "Samuel! Samuel!"

Then Samuel said, "Speak, for your servant is listening."

11 And the LORD said to Samuel: "See, I am about to do something in Israel that will make the ears of everyone who hears of it tingle.

Samuel believed in the Lord and became a great prophet.

Your trust in God is rewarding.

Hope is empowered by the Holy Spirit.

Romans 15:13

13 May the God of hope fill you with all joy and peace as you trust in him, so that you may overflow with hope by the power of the Holy Spirit.

1 John 4:13-16

13 We know that we live in him and he in us, because he has given us of his Spirit. 14 And we have seen and testify that the Father has sent his Son to be the Savior of the world. 15 If anyone acknowledges that Jesus is the Son of God, God lives in him and he in God. 16 And so we know and rely on the love God has for us.

POINTS OF INTEREST

1. Have you heard God call you like this?

2. What was your trust level at His beckon?

3. We can trust in God's love for us.

WORD OF WISDOM

Here is what happens when they do and don't trust the Lord.

Jerimiah 7:23-24

23 But this thing commanded I them, saying, Obey my voice, and I will be your God, and ye shall be my people: and walk ye in all the ways that I have commanded you, that it may be well unto you.

24 But they hearkened not, nor inclined their ear, but walked in the counsels and in the imagination of their evil heart, and went backward, and not forward. KJV

Wait upon the Lord

An old favorite song from this verse rings in my ears. Although it is still true. As I get older it becomes more relevant, the meaning is accurate for all ages.

Isaiah 40:31

31 But they that wait upon the LORD shall renew their strength; they shall mount up with wings as eagles; they shall run, and not be weary; and they shall walk, and not faint. KJV   Help me Lord, help me Lord to wait."

Waiting on the Lord has to do with being patient for His answer and action. God's judgment is timely, better, and comprehensive when we want it now. Our impatience is incomplete and short-sighted.

Being patient for Him gives us time to gather our wits and godly character, for a better perspective to let love and forgiveness work their generosity.

Waiting on the Lord can take years for the answer to come to completeness. The promise of a ministry that takes realistic preparation for one to be ready. All the time we should nurture the promise with faith and hope to keep it alive until we are trusted with the position. This allows time for correction and direction of the ministry along with strengthening the vision. The Holy Spirit will help you wait.

I know a guy who joined the army to get training for a missionary position but turned it into a secular job when he got out. I was a bit disappointed because I thought he would be a great missionary.

Another thing that I think is important, is that when the vision begins to get dim, it's time to ask the Lord to reinvigorate the vision or remove it because that could be a lot of time spent on the wrong track. Or even worse would be that the vision fades and never comes back or returns too late. Many good visions are lost to something less valuable. Often money pulls them out of God's will. What a shame. So, if there is a hint of doubt, quickly ask the Lord to revise the power of Hope to revive the dreams.

When we wait upon the Lord, we should be like an attentive restaurant waiter who moves quickly when they understand what the customer wants. Their job is to please the customer. They are intently focused on the patron's desires. Attend to the Lord's desires.

POINTS OF INTEREST

1. How do you wait upon the Lord?
2. Do you have a dream that has faded?
3. What do you do if you forget the dream?

WORD OF WISDOM

What happens to a person that walks away from their God-given dream?

Proverbs 29:18

18 Where there is no vision, the people perish: but he that keepeth the law, happy is he. KJV

If a country walks away from the Lord, it could be disastrous.

A person may not die, but they could have a more fulfilling life going the way the Lord wants.

Fruitfulness

The fruit of faith in Christ is the realization of pure faith, hope, and trust in the Lord.

Psalms 1:1-3

Blessed is the man

who does not walk in the counsel of the wicked

or stand in the way of sinners

or sit in the seat of mockers.

2 But his delight is in the law of the LORD,

and on his law he meditates day and night.

3 He is like a tree planted by streams of water,

which yields its fruit in season

and whose leaf does not wither.

Whatever he does prosper.

This guy has wisdom, knowledge, and understanding which was birthed from the fear of the Lord. This is like a professionally cut expensive diamond. Each facet is polished at the perfect angle to reflect the light dazzlingly.

We strive to live up to this description as Jesus did by keeping attached to the vine, Jesus, who lived His life blamelessly before the Father.

Psalms 15

LORD, who may dwell in your sanctuary?

Who may live on your holy hill?

2 He whose walk is blameless and who does what is righteous,

who speaks the truth from his heart

3 and has no slander on his tongue,

who does his neighbor no wrong

and casts no slur on his fellowman,

4 who despises a vile man but honors those who fear the LORD, who keeps his oath even when it hurts,

5 who lends his money without usury and does not accept a bribe against the innocent. He who does these things will never be shaken.

I need to reside in your presence Jesus so I can be fruitful in your Kingdom.

Psalms 27:4-5

4 one thing I ask of the LORD,

this is what I seek:

that I may dwell in the house of the LORD

all the days of my life,

to gaze upon the beauty of the LORD

and to seek him in his temple.

5 For in the day of trouble

he will keep me safe in his dwelling;

he will hide me in the shelter of his tabernacle

and set me high upon a rock.

How must I prepare to come into your presence, Jesus?

Psalms 24:3-6

3 Who may ascend the hill of the LORD?

Who may stand in his holy place?

4 He who has clean hands and a pure heart,

who does not lift up his soul to an idol

or swear by what is false.

5 He will receive blessing from the LORD

and vindication from God his Savior.

6 Such is the generation of those who seek him,

who seek your face, O God of Jacob.

The psalmist describes the Lord as the destination of our determined effort to be made into His image.

Psalms 145

I will exalt you, my God the King; I will praise your name for ever and ever. 2 Every day I will praise you and extol your name for ever and ever.

3 Great is the LORD and most worthy of praise; his greatness no one can fathom. 4 one generation will commend your works to another; they will tell of your mighty acts. 5 They will speak of the glorious splendor of your majesty, and I will meditate on your wonderful works. 6 They will tell of the power of your awesome works, and I will proclaim your great deeds. 7 They will celebrate your abundant goodness and joyfully sing of your righteousness.

8 The LORD is gracious and compassionate, slow to anger and rich in love. 9 The LORD is good to all; he has compassion on all he has made. 10 All you have made will praise you, O LORD; your saints will extol you. 11 They will tell of the glory of your kingdom and speak of your might, 12 so that all men may know of your mighty acts

and the glorious splendor of your kingdom. 13 Your kingdom is an everlasting kingdom, and your dominion endures through all generations.

The LORD is faithful to all his promises and loving toward all he has made.   14 The LORD upholds all those who fall and lifts up all who are bowed down. 15 The eyes of all look to you, and you give them their food at the proper time. 16 You open your hand and satisfy the desires of every living thing.

17 The LORD is righteous in all his ways and loving toward all he has made. 18 The LORD is near to all who call on him, to all who call on him in truth. 19 He fulfills the desires of those who fear him; he hears their cry and saves them. 20 The LORD watches over all who love him, but all the wicked he will destroy.

21 My mouth will speak in praise of the LORD. Let every creature praise his holy name for ever and ever.

Lord, we glorify and exalt you forever for your great grace, for your accepting us by forgiveness and inclusion into your Kingdom, King Jesus. We are most grateful.

We dedicate the fruit of the seed you planted in our hearts as an offering to you.

Please accept this fruit from your imputed righteousness, that we have laid on the altar of your presence. We give you our heartfelt thanksgiving.

Humble yourself before the Lord.

Ephesians 4:1-6

4:1 As a prisoner for the Lord, then, I urge you to live a life worthy of the calling you have received. 2 Be completely humble and gentle; be patient, bearing with one another in love. 3 Make every effort to keep the unity of the Spirit through the bond of peace. 4 There is one body and one Spirit- just as you were called to one hope when you were called- 5 one Lord, one faith, one baptism; 6 one God and Father of all, who is over all and through all and in all.

Keep Jesus' life your goal for your life.

POINTS OF INTEREST

1. What is the importance of being humble?
2. What does James say about being humble?
3. What don't you like about humbling yourself?
4. What happens if you don't humble yourself?

James 4:5-10

5 Or do you think Scripture says without reason that the spirit he caused to live in us envies intensely? 6 But he gives us more grace. That is why Scripture says:

"God opposes the proud

but gives grace to the humble."

7 Submit yourselves, then, to God. Resist the devil, and he will flee from you. 8 Come near to God and he will come near to you. Wash your hands, you sinners, and purify your hearts, you double-minded. 9 Grieve, mourn and wail. Change your laughter to mourning and your joy to gloom. 10 Humble yourselves before the Lord, and he will lift you up.

WORD OF WISDOM

Do what it takes to cause your body to be fruitful for the Kingdom of God.

Daniel 10:12-13

12 Then he continued, "Do not be afraid, Daniel. Since the first day that you set your mind to gain understanding and to humble yourself before your God, your words were heard, and I have come in response to them.

Believe

To believe is a powerful process. It enlightens your spirit with different knowledge and understanding that can change your whole mindset and direction in life. It can change your DNA and your destiny. Your heart, soul, and spirit need to make sure that this is the best way to go. The Holy Spirit will give its firm certification if you ask. "Yes, this is true." The renewing of the mind changes you.

Belief lives in the same house as Hope, just in different rooms. Jesus says to believe in Him and you will be saved. There is no more powerful act that a person can do. Just by changing your mind from not believing to believing in Jesus, it takes you off the road to Hell to put you on the road to Heaven instantly. And now you belong to Jesus forever. He will change His righteousness for your unrighteousness so now you can communicate with the Father, which fulfills His heart. Father God cannot allow unrighteousness in His presence. So, with Jesus' righteousness in your heart, you are accepted in the presence of God for prayer and direction, for the Holy Spirit, who is the Spirit of God. And that fulfills the purpose that the Godhead had at the beginning of sending Jesus to come down to earth and die for our sins and bridging the death chasm between life and death for us. He took the punishment for us sinners so we wouldn't have to die in Hell for our sins. Belief is the key and the power to enter life in the Kingdom of God, breaking down an impassable barrier. You can't do any better than that.

Pride is a wall that you must break down to get to the humble side before the Lord God almighty who made Heaven and earth, and is the final judge, and be saved.

You may think that just belief is too easy to be forgiven, but God is merciful and gracious to us mere humans. He knows that we are made of dust and He loves us and His creation.

Acts 2:38-39

38 Peter replied, "Repent and be baptized, every one of you, in the name of Jesus Christ for the forgiveness of your sins. And you will receive the gift of the Holy Spirit. 39 The promise is for you and your children and for all who are far off-for all whom the Lord our God will call."

In this instant, Jesus will exchange His righteousness for your unrighteousness so you will be accepted into the presence of God to communicate with Him forever.

Blessed are those who have believed and not seen.

John 20:29

29 Then Jesus told him, "Because you have seen me, you have believed; blessed are those who have not seen and yet have believed."

It is the same type of miracle in metamorphous as a worm turning into a butterfly, or a tadpole turning into a frog. A lot of things have to change, especially in your thinking. Believing Jesus to become your Lord and savior changes who you are and where you are going. You become a child of God and you are going to Heaven and not Hell.

When I was saved at the Assembly of God's youth camp, I came home with a different spirit that I understood. At eleven years old, I realized that I wanted to be righteous because Jesus wanted that in me also. It is still real to me because I remember some incidents that are still effective in my life seventy-four years later. Some Sunday school stories are still active in my mind. I count them precious. For half a lifetime, I am still refining this righteousness.

Then the responsibility rests on us to press in and learn more about this Jesus. These lessons will guide your life to follow after the Life of Jesus and be transformed into the image of Jesus, and be fruitful in His kingdom. Many years later I am still growing in righteousness, looking forward to being made in the likeness of Jesus.

Matthew 11:28-30

28 Come unto me, all ye that labour and are heavy laden, and I will give you rest.

29 Take my yoke upon you, and learn of me; for I am meek and lowly in heart: and ye shall find rest unto your souls.

30 For my yoke is easy, and my burden is light. KJV

The new Christian now dances to a different tune and obeys a different master.

Romans 4:18-25

18 Against all hope, Abraham in hope believed and so became the father of many nations, just as it had been said to him, "So shall your offspring be." 19 Without weakening in his faith, he faced the fact that his body was as good as dead-since he was about a hundred years old-and that Sarah's womb was also dead. 20 Yet he did not waver through unbelief regarding the promise of God, but was strengthened in his faith and gave glory to God, 21 being fully persuaded that God had power to do what he had promised. 22 This is why "it was credited to him as righteousness." 23 The words "it was credited to him" were written not for him alone, 24 but also for us, to whom God will credit righteousness-for us who believe in him who raised Jesus our Lord from the dead. 25 He was delivered over to death for our sins and was raised to life for our justification.

We should also be patient with the Lord while He is in the process of bringing His agenda to happen in our lives. I have gone through many patient tests to bring me to an improved waiting on Him. I cherish these tests because I know their eternal value.

Of Abraham's own volition he elected to put his confidence in the word of the Lord to not disbelieve but to positively put his trust in what he heard God say.

This belief in God changed Abraham and all his children, natural and spiritual, and the believers in God who had this same faith to be made righteous.

Romans 3:19-26

19 Now we know that whatever the law says, it says to those who are under the law, so that every mouth may be silenced and the whole world held accountable to God. 20 Therefore no one will be declared righteous in his sight by observing the law; rather, through the law we become conscious of sin.

21 But now a righteousness from God, apart from law, has been made known, to which the Law and the Prophets testify. 22 This righteousness from God comes through faith in Jesus Christ to all who believe. There is no difference, 23 for all have sinned and fall short of the glory of God, 24 and are justified freely by his grace through the redemption that came by Christ Jesus. 25 God presented him as a sacrifice of atonement, through faith in his blood. He did this to demonstrate his justice, because in his forbearance he had left the sins committed beforehand unpunished- 26 he did it to demonstrate his justice at the present time, so as to be just and the one who justifies those who have faith in Jesus.

Our faith in Jesus justifies us.

Galatians 3:5-9

5 Does God give you his Spirit and work miracles among you because you observe the law, or because you believe what you heard?

6 Consider Abraham: "He believed God, and it was credited to him as righteousness." 7 Understand, then, that those who believe are children of Abraham. 8 The Scripture foresaw that God would justify the Gentiles by faith, and announced the gospel in advance to Abraham: "All nations will be blessed through you." 9 So those who have faith are blessed along with Abraham, the man of faith.

In order for a person to believe there needs to be a point of contact. The best beginning is in the fear of the Lord. For out of the state of mind comes the ability to even approach God. Somehow a person needs to have some idea of the relevance of God to receive the respect and reverence of God. I believe this comes out of that small measure of faith that God puts into every baby that He makes.

Every young person is built with an eagerness to learn, so they are ready to learn about their maker. I began to learn about Jesus at about the age of 7 as my grandmother would talk to me about Jesus. She planted and watered that seed until church camp when I was led to invite Him into my heart and that seed blossomed. I knew this because I obeyed what my grandmother and Sunday school teacher taught me, and I was a righteous little kid.

As long as I lived with my grandparents I did well in the Lord until my mother, brother and I moved to another town. There went my stabilizing force, and I was on my own. I had a hard time learning about society without my Christian grandparents. Fourteen years later I divorced from a bad marriage. But the wonderful ten formative years with my grandparents came back to me and I ran back into the Kingdom like a hungry prodigal and never looked back. I had only about one hour of post-partum blues about the loss of my family when I was divorced and then I was on top higher than ever before. God was most gracious to me.

POINTS OF INTEREST

1.   What happens in your mind when you believe?
2.   Tell me how easy salvation is.
3.   What is the hard part of being a Christian?

WORD OF WISDOM

Ask Jesus to help you when you have some unbelief.

Mark 9:21-27

"From childhood," he answered. 22 "It has often thrown him into fire or water to kill him. But if you can do anything, take pity on us and help us."

23 "'If you can'?" said Jesus. "Everything is possible for him who believes."

24 Immediately the boy's father exclaimed, "I do believe; help me overcome my unbelief!"

25 When Jesus saw that a crowd was running to the scene, he rebuked the evil spirit. "You deaf and mute spirit," he said, "I command you, come out of him and never enter him again."

26 The spirit shrieked, convulsed him violently and came out. The boy looked so much like a corpse that many said, "He's dead." 27 But Jesus took him by the hand and lifted him to his feet, and he stood up.

Justification

Justification feels comfortable in my spirit, and my heart smiles when I am validated. It makes life worthwhile being somebody. The Love of Jesus gives me hope for tomorrow.

The book of Romans 4;25 says, He was delivered over to death for our sins and was raised to life for our justification.

Jesus was raised by the power of God so we could be justified. This was the proof of the sovereign God using that power to eradicate our sins because we believe in Jesus. Justified - Just as if we had never sinned. That is awesome power over my soul. The negative memory and effect of my past sins have been wiped clean like a whiteboard. An added benefit is that our DNA has been realigned unto blameless.

When a person is justified, they are considered to be right and worthy of righteousness. So, in the act of believing in Jesus, a person has acted with faith that Jesus is whom He said He is and is justified in their heart. Along with the power of Hope and the step of trust in our understanding, we receive salvation. The process of renewing the mind moves us into the new person realm so we can go out into the world to conquer, be victorious, and be successful wherever the Lord leads.

Heart and words are triumphant.

Romans 10:8-10

8 But what does it say? "The word is near you; it is in your mouth and in your heart," that is, the word of faith we are proclaiming: 9 That if you confess with your mouth, "Jesus is Lord," and believe in your heart that God raised him from the dead, you will be saved. 10 For it is with your heart that you believe and are justified, and it is with your mouth that you confess and are saved.

This is also a faith, hope, and trust progression.

To demonstrate salvation, one must believe deep in their heart that Jesus is the only one who can save you. Hope adds power from your heart, then trust that you can say with your mouth that He is your Lord, and you are saved. Your mind and mouth must agree together to make it a fact. The soul and spirit must be settled on this detail. Then the process of making Jesus Lord of your life begins. Trust kicks in and you begin to witness your new faith in Jesus, by telling somebody. Lord means that He tells you what to do, what to say, how to act, and when you obey it. Just saying the words to be saved is not fact until you can truthfully say from your heart, "Jesus is Lord."

Jesus is the one who baptizes you in the Holy Spirit to help you to learn and obey the commands of Jesus. With the Holy Spirit in your heart, you have better access to God the Father, and instructions on how to live your life. You can now speak to Him and Him through you in a language you don't understand, or your own language, and that He interprets to the Father to do the business of the Kingdom of God. Then it is a prayer that He can answer.

Acts 2:5-9

5 Now there were staying in Jerusalem God-fearing Jews from every nation under heaven. 6 When they heard this sound, a crowd came together in bewilderment, because each one heard them speaking in his own language. 7 Utterly amazed, they asked: "Are not all these men who are speaking Galileans? 8 Then how is it that each of us hears them in his own native language? 9 Parthians, Medes and Elamites; residents of Mesopotamia, Judea and Cappadocia, Pontus and Asia, of Mesopotamia, Judea and Cappadocia, Pontus and Asia,

Paul's call to speak in tongues.

1 Corinthians 14:1-5

14:1 Follow the way of love and eagerly desire spiritual gifts, especially the gift of prophecy. 2 For anyone who speaks in a tongue does not speak to men but to God. Indeed, no one understands him; he utters mysteries with his spirit. 3 But everyone who prophesies speaks to men for their strengthening, encouragement and comfort. 4 He who speaks in a tongue edifies himself, but he who prophesies edifies the church. 5 I would like every one of you to speak in tongues, but I would rather have you prophesy. He who prophesies is greater than one who speaks in tongues, unless he interprets, so that the church may be edified.

The full communication with God by the Holy Spirit.

When Jesus comes into your life, the Father and Holy Spirit come in also. To complete the union, Jesus takes you into the Holy Spirit for full communion.

This newly imputed righteousness is free to you by receiving salvation, and this righteousness will give you access to the Father for communication. Until this time, one doesn't meaningly hear from God. And then by the Holy Spirit's help, you work on experiential righteousness through many lessons and tests that will enable you to come to the image of Christ, the Righteousness of God. It might take a lifetime.

Don't forget where you came from, and how high God has lifted you up to be seated with Him. Humble yourself because He has taken you from being apart from God to being seated with Him by justifying you with His mighty grace. He didn't have to save and justify you; He wanted to through His love, grace, and the shed blood of Jesus on the cross.

Romans 3:21-28

21 But now a righteousness from God, apart from law, has been made known, to which the Law and the Prophets testify. 22 This righteousness from God comes through faith in Jesus Christ to all who believe. There is no difference, 23 for all have sinned and fall short of the glory of God, 24 and are justified freely by his grace through the redemption that came by Christ Jesus. 25 God presented him as a sacrifice of atonement, through faith in his blood. He did this to demonstrate his justice, because in his forbearance he had left the sins committed beforehand unpunished- 26 he did it to demonstrate his justice at the present time, so as to be just and the one who justifies those who have faith in Jesus.

27 Where, then, is boasting? It is excluded. On what principle? On that of observing the law? No, but on that of faith. 28 For we maintain that a man is justified by faith apart from observing the law.

Abram had faith in God that He would do what He said He would, and He hoped for ten years, or so, for the promise of a son. His effectual hope was steadfast and he trusted the word of God and had a son in his old age. For this God ascribed Abraham to righteousness. God justified Abe for following through with the promise given to him.

Romans 4:1-6

4:1 What then shall we say that Abraham, our forefather, discovered in this matter? 2 If, in fact, Abraham was justified by works, he had something to boast about-but not before God. 3 What does the Scripture say? "Abraham believed God, and it was credited to him as righteousness."

4 Now when a man works, his wages are not credited to him as a gift, but as an obligation. 5 However, to the man

who does not work but trusts God who justifies the wicked, his faith is credited as righteousness. 6 David says the same thing when he speaks of the blessedness of the man to whom God credits righteousness apart from works:

Now that we have been justified through faith, we have access to God, His peace, and real hope for the glory of God. He is so gracious.

Romans 5:1-5

5:1 Therefore, since we have been justified through faith, we have peace with God through our Lord Jesus Christ, 2 through whom we have gained access by faith into this grace in which we now stand. And we rejoice in the hope of the glory of God. 3 Not only so, but we also rejoice in our sufferings, because we know that suffering produces perseverance; 4 perseverance, character; and character, hope. 5 And hope does not disappoint us, because God has poured out his love into our hearts by the Holy Spirit, whom he has given us.

The hope of the glory of God

When you learn what the glory of God is and what it is like, you will want it and will do what it takes to get there. The Glory of God is wrapped up in His greatness in love, deeds, ability, and all he does and has made. Through Jesus Christ, He invites us to partake and experience all that is in Him, by Him, and through Him. He wants us to be one with Him.

We rejoice in our sufferings,

To the normal person, it sounds ridiculous to rejoice when you suffer, but when the Lord takes you through suffering you will find out it's a good thing because the results are for your good.

Jesus had to suffer; why should we do anything less?

Hebrews 2:8-9

In putting everything under him, God left nothing that is not subject to him. Yet at present we do not see everything subject to him. 9 But we see Jesus, who was made a little lower than the angels, now crowned with glory and honor because he suffered death, so that by the grace of God he might taste death for everyone.

I am sad Jesus had to suffer, but I'm grateful He did it for me.

Hebrews 5:8-9

8 Although he was a son, he learned obedience from what he suffered 9 and, once made perfect, he became the source of eternal salvation for all who obey him

There is a bit of suffering every time we learn something important.

Perseverance

Some of us are impetuous and impulsive, anxious and apprehensive, and so on, so we need help. Giving up is our middle name, but God's middle name is long-suffering and He wants us to give it to us. We need this ability so we can wait on Him. One of my greatest tests is patience. I just want to do it and get it done, but this shortcut is a critical part of schooling. That essential element is perseverance. What a drag, Do you mean you want it done perfectly? Maybe, I'm tired of this task? One guy said, "If it is worth doing, it's worth doing well." Thoroughness is a Kingdom of God quality. God never does things halfway. So, buckle up; this may take a little more time to get it right. God made Creation right from the smallest to the largest item, from the elements in the air to the elements in the universe, because they must all work together. He persevered until it was perfect.

Character

The Holy Spirit knows what our character is like and what it should be like and establishes a curriculum to take us through a course to make us look more like Jesus so that He can draw more people to Him.

We are ambassadors for the Lord through this extreme sacrifice.

2 Corinthians 5:16-21

17 Therefore, if anyone is in Christ, he is a new creation; the old has gone, the new has come! 18 All this is from God, who reconciled us to himself through Christ and gave us the ministry of reconciliation: 19 that God was reconciling the world to himself in Christ, not counting men's sins against them. And he has committed to us the message of reconciliation. 20 We are therefore Christ's ambassadors, as though God were making his appeal through us. We implore you on Christ's behalf: Be reconciled to God. 21 God made him who had no sin to be sin for us so that in him we might become the righteousness of God.

God wants our characters to reflect Him, as they purposed in Creation.

Genesis 1:26-27

26 Then God said, "Let us make man in our image, in our likeness, and let them rule over the fish of the sea and the birds of the air, over the livestock, over all the earth, and over all the creatures that move along the ground."

27 So God created man in his own image, in the image of God he created him;

male and female he created them.

But man fell into sin and the long road of reconciliation began.

Jesus looks like He could be our uncle. The only difference is the character, and He is working on that. We are born in the world and from earthly parents who were not perfect, so Christ-like character is a priority improvement project. This too is progress to bring us closer to Him. This side track is not outside the rebuilding procedure, but it is integral.

I look at my divorce as a reasonable result of my lack of Christian knowledge of marriage. I married a non-Christian and lived ten years moving away from my Christian roots. I couldn't handle not going to church, not reading the Bible, not tithing, or even talking about Jesus. I got kicked out of the bedroom and slept in my little daughter's portable bed for the next eighteen years. We were married only ten years. The little bed went with me from a cabin to the second bedroom of my friend to an empty house, to a Christian house for ministry, to another friend's second bedroom, to another friend's basement, to the basement of an empty rented home for me and a couple of friends. At this house, I traded roommates and married a Christian, Roberta, and kicked those guys out. I had to get a bigger bed.

I see the Lord's hand on my life. "Since you chose not to listen to your grandmother who told you not to marry a non-Christion, I took you to a path that would lead you the way I want you to go." During those fourteen years, I had to pay up to half my take-home pay for child support, so I learned to live quite leanly.

I learned a lot of valuable character lessons, and I wouldn't trade them for anything. I feel that I would have been better off had I married a Christian in the first place.

I can certainly feel grateful and know God's justification, 'just as if I had never sinned' clause in the agreement.

hope

Suffering teaches in ways that can't be done any other way. I appreciate the Lord taking me the long way to get me where He wants me. I am now dedicated to Him and His righteousness. A precious destination. But I am still somewhat of a character, I credit my heritage for that.

This hope does not disappoint us, but we are encouraged when we recognize that we are better off for going through trials.

Our hope in God is that we Christians glory in God, and we are glorified in God knowing that He will lift us up to where He is, and this is the best we can hope to attain too. The Holy Spirit will confirm this fact in our hearts.

1 Peter 1:13-21

13 Therefore, prepare your minds for action; be self-controlled; set your hope fully on the grace to be given you when Jesus Christ is revealed. 14 As obedient children, do not conform to the evil desires you had when you lived in ignorance. 15 But just as he who called you is holy, so be holy in all you do; 16 for it is written: "Be holy, because I am holy."

17 Since you call on a Father who judges each man's work impartially, live your lives as strangers here in reverent fear. 18 For you know that it was not with perishable things such as silver or gold that you were redeemed from the empty way of life handed down to you from your forefathers, 19 but with the precious blood of Christ, a lamb without blemish or defect. 20 He was chosen before the creation of the world, but was revealed in these last times for your sake. 21 Through him you believe in God, who

raised him from the dead and glorified him, and so your faith and hope are in God.

Our hope carries us into the heavenly because of what God does for us like justification and presents us as righteous before all Heavens.

Our hope in Jesus carries us way above the laws of Moses and could bring us to erase all our sins and iniquities forever. Thank you, Jesus, for fulfilling the Laws of Moses.

Acts 13:38-39

38 "Therefore, my brothers, I want you to know that through Jesus the forgiveness of sins is proclaimed to you. 39 Through him everyone who believes is justified from everything you could not be justified from by the law of Moses.

With the coming of Jesus, we are much better off than those who had only the laws of Moses. His death took care of the penalty of sin for us as He instituted the law of justice for believers. And He also instituted glorification for our justification.

Romans 8:28-30

28 And we know that in all things God works for the good of those who love him, who have been called according to his purpose. 29 For those God foreknew he also predestined to be conformed to the likeness of his Son, that he might be the firstborn among many brothers. 30 And those he predestined, he also called; those he called, he also justified; those he justified, he also glorified.

I am so glad that God is so detailed that He sees and works all these 'not so good things I go through, out for my good for me. I truly do love Him.

There is coming a day of hope for total glorification for those who believe in Jesus and His justification.

2 Thessalonians 1:10

10 on the day he comes to be glorified in his holy people and to be marveled at among all those who have believed. This includes you because you believed our testimony to you.

POINTS OF INTEREST

1. What is so good about believing without seeing?

2. Explain how you feel being justified before God.

3. Do you also hope in His glorification?

WORD OF WISDOM

Believing in Jesus sight unseen is to be commended.

1 Peter 1:3-9

3 Praise be to the God and Father of our Lord Jesus Christ! In his great mercy he has given us new birth into a living hope through the resurrection of Jesus Christ from the dead, 4 and into an inheritance that can never perish, spoil or fade-kept in heaven for you, 5 who through faith are shielded by God's power until the coming of the salvation that is ready to be revealed in the last time. 6 In this you greatly rejoice, though now for a little while you may have had to suffer grief in all kinds of trials. 7 These have come so that your faith-of greater worth than gold, which perishes even though refined by fire-may be proved genuine and may result in praise, glory and honor when Jesus Christ is revealed. 8 Though you have not seen him, you love him; and even though you do not see him now, you believe in him and are filled with an inexpressible and glorious joy, 9 for you are receiving the goal of your faith, the salvation of your souls.

Sanctification

The setting aside, especially for a purpose.

We set ourselves aside for the Lord by the word of truth, the Bible.

When I came back to Jesus, I did everything I knew to sanctify myself to the Lord. It only took an hour to go from my lowest point to my high point in the Lord when my family left. I knew that I needed to go to church, pray, read the Bible, and tithe, so I immediately turned the corner. I knew how to set my life in the world aside and pursue the Christian way for I had some good training when I was young. Sanctification was the only way I wanted to go. The perfect opportunity presented itself, so I was off to see the Kingdom and I have never looked back after 56 years.

The pursuit increases in intent and in sanctification. Even in writing this book, I am trying to increase my fear of the Lord, which is respect and reverence for the Lord. How can I obey and esteem Him more in my morality and profound worship? It's always on my mind.

John 17:15-19

16 They are not of the world, even as I am not of it. 17 Sanctify them by the truth; your word is truth. 18 As you sent me into the world, I have sent them into the world. 19 For them I sanctify myself, that they too may be truly sanctified.

We must be cleansed by the Holy Spirit, God's spirit.

Romans 15:14-16

15 I have written you quite boldly on some points, as if to remind you of them again, because of the grace God gave me 16 to be a minister of Christ Jesus to the Gentiles with the priestly duty of proclaiming the gospel of God, so that

the Gentiles might become an offering acceptable to God, sanctified by the Holy Spirit.

Washing spiritually aids in setting yourself aside for the Lord.

1 Corinthians 6:9-11

9 Do you not know that the wicked will not inherit the kingdom of God? Do not be deceived: Neither the sexually immoral nor idolaters nor adulterers nor male prostitutes nor homosexual offenders 10 nor thieves nor the greedy nor drunkards nor slanderers nor swindlers will inherit the kingdom of God. 11 And that is what some of you were. But you were washed, you were sanctified, you were justified in the name of the Lord Jesus Christ and by the Spirit of our God.

Cleansed from immorality to be sanctified by God, by knowing God obediently and all that implies. For God is pure and we are to be pure and be consecrated to Him.

God has called us to be unpolluted and sacred to Him to be sanctified. The Holy Spirit will discipline you through the process. Ask for His help because He wants you pure.

1 Thessalonians 4:3-8

3 It is God's will that you should be sanctified: that you should avoid sexual immorality; 4 that each of you should learn to control his own body in a way that is holy and honorable, 5 not in passionate lust like the heathen, who do not know God; 6 and that in this matter no one should wrong his brother or take advantage of him. The Lord will punish men for all such sins, as we have already told you and warned you. 7 For God did not call us to be impure, but to live a holy life. 8 Therefore, he who rejects this instruction does not reject man but God, who gives you his Holy Spirit.

POINTS OF INTEREST

1. What does it take to live a holy life?

2. Explain sanctified.

3. What are some of the ways to be sanctified?

4. How do you dedicate yourself to the Lord?

5. How do you set yourself aside to the Lord?

6. What do you not do to sanctify yourself to the Lord?

WORD OF WISDOM

Once you were not sanctified, but now you are.

1 Corinthians 1:2

2 To the church of God in Corinth, to those sanctified in Christ Jesus and called to be holy, together with all those everywhere who call on the name of our Lord Jesus Christ-their Lord and ours:

Truth

Some have asked if I write nonfiction. And I say, "I don't like to read it because you can't believe what it says, and I don't want stuff in my mind that is not pure and true. It might confuse or dilute some good stuff that is in there that I don't want to be muffled. If it ain't true, I don't want it. There is no use confusing or diluting my soul and spirit.

My friend said to throw the evil words and thoughts into the sea of forgetfulness and put up a sign that says, "No fishing."

Jesus claimed that He was the truth because He came from God who is His Father, and His Father's only-begotten Son. How that works is a mystery to us humans because we are ignorant about these truths, and have no references outside of the Lord.

Since the Holy Spirit came down to Jesus as a dove and remained on Him, He was filled with the Holy Spirit. He was able to be tested to the max and start His earthly ministry. Up until then, Jesus was led and trained by the Spirit of God, the written word, and upright parents. Jesus had come to the point that He knew that He was the way, the truth, and the life that was the only way to God. As the Holy Spirit trained Jesus, the Spirit trains us also. Jesus had the Holy Spirit at birth.

Jesus would purposefully get away and pray at night when it was quiet and the disciples were asleep. We need to find time to be with the Lord alone so we can get some intimate training. The Holy Spirit doesn't sleep so we can talk to Him at all hours. Find a habit you can get into with Him.

Jesus said this because he images the Father's being.

Jesus is the truth and He came to earth to tell us the truth about the Father.

John 18:37

37 "You are a king, then!" said Pilate.

Jesus answered, "You are right in saying I am a king. In fact, for this reason I was born, and for this I came into the world, to testify to the truth. Everyone on the side of truth listens to me."

Everything Jesus said was the truth because He could not lie because God cannot lie and the Father and the Son are in the same mind. God's truthfulness is an anchor for our souls. When we are tied to God as the truth, we won't drift away into our own imagination that would take our minds detaching from His reality.

Hebrews 6:16-20

16 Men swear by someone greater than themselves, and the oath confirms what is said and puts an end to all argument. 17 Because God wanted to make the unchanging nature of his purpose very clear to the heirs of what was promised, he confirmed it with an oath. 18 God did this so that, by two unchangeable things in which it is impossible for God to lie, we who have fled to take hold of the hope offered to us may be greatly encouraged. 19 We have this hope as an anchor for the soul, firm and secure. It enters the inner sanctuary behind the curtain, 20 where Jesus, who went before us, has entered on our behalf. He has become a high priest forever, in the order of Melchizedek.

Jesus learned from the scriptures and from the Voice of the Father and the Spirit of God.

The Bible is the restraint that keeps us firmly attached to the mooring of the Lord. It is up to us to keep it in good repair by reading, hearing, meditating, and studying it until it is in our mouths and at the forefront of our minds. The Bible must be kept fresh so that the tainted words and thoughts of the world will always be caught in this filter of the truth.

Then your thinking will be a compiling of true words to shield you from wrong thoughts and present an avenue for the Holy Spirit to proclaim the pure Gospel. Before I read the Bible I didn't have very much to say. Then I purposed to read and study the Bible a lot. This gave me words and purpose along with the boldness to speak.

I read through the Bible in about a year and a half, turn it over and continue again from Genesis. I have had an everyday regiment since 1966 and I am still learning.

POINTS OF INTEREST

1. How do you feel about truth?

2. How do you know when you are filled with the Holy Spirit?

3. What part of you gets agitated when you hear a lie?

4. How do you build a fortress against untruth?

WORD OF WISDOM

Truth brings the freedom to live in faith, hope, and trust.

Psalms 119:30-32

30 I have chosen the way of truth;

I have set my heart on your laws.

31 I hold fast to your statutes, O LORD;

do not let me be put to shame.

32 I run in the path of your commands,

for you have set my heart free.

The power of God

God's power is involved in everything created. He created the heavens and the earth and everything in it. He created all things large and small, seen and unseen, attitudes and rules, and He still knows all and is in control. He keeps everything going by His power.

I am becoming aware more and more of the miraculous works and power. I am hearing the prophets and seeing the fulfillment of their prophecy, increasing my hope. I see the answers to my prayers and faith is encouraged. I am seeing His Kingdom expand and I trust for more. I rejoice in my expectancy of the Glory of God. I am confident God will answer my prayers, so I continue to pray.

Don't stop praying because you didn't see your particular prayer answered immediately, He heard it. He answers some right away and some later, be patient with Him, as He is patient with you.

Romans 1:20

20 For since the creation of the world God's invisible qualities-his eternal power and divine nature-have been clearly seen, being understood from what has been made, so that men are without excuse.

God gives power to whomever He wants like Samson.

Judges 14:6

6 The Spirit of the LORD came upon him in power so that he tore the lion apart with his bare hands as he might have torn a young goat. But he told neither his father nor his mother what he had done.

In the Old Testament, the Spirit would come on individuals to complete a task and then leave. In the New Testament, first, the Holy Spirit came down to Mary to conceive Jesus, then on Jesus like a dove, and remained when John baptized Him. Now Jesus is the one who can baptize people in the Holy Spirit.

John 1:32-33

32 Then John gave this testimony: "I saw the Spirit come down from heaven as a dove and remain on him. 33 I would not have known him, except that the one who sent me to baptize with water told me, 'The man on whom you see the Spirit come down and remain is he who will baptize with the Holy Spirit.'

Then the Holy Spirit was poured out on all flesh.

Acts 2:1-4

2:1 When the day of Pentecost came, they were all together in one place. 2 Suddenly a sound like the blowing of a violent wind came from heaven and filled the whole house where they were sitting. 3 They saw what seemed to be tongues of fire that separated and came to rest on each of them. 4 All of them were filled with the Holy Spirit and began to speak in other tongues as the Spirit enabled them.

With their new boldness, Peter started a Jesus movement, but this newfound power to witness by the Holy Spirit.

Acts 2:14-18

14 Then Peter stood up with the eleven, raised his voice and addressed the crowd: "Fellow Jews and all of you who live in Jerusalem, let me explain this to you; listen carefully to what I say. 15 These men are not drunk, as you suppose. It's only nine in the morning! 16 No, this is what was spoken by the prophet Joel:

17 "'In the last days, God says, I will pour out my Spirit on all people.

Your sons and daughters will prophesy, your young men will see visions,

your old men will dream dreams.

18 Even on my servants, both men and women, I will pour out my Spirit in those days, and they will prophesy

The Holy Spirit was also giving him words and eloquence.

Jesus continues to baptize men and women in the Holy Spirit today.

Acts 2:32-33

32 God has raised this Jesus to life, and we are all witnesses of the fact. 33 Exalted to the right hand of God, he has received from the Father the promised Holy Spirit and has poured out what you now see and hear.

POINTS OF INTEREST

1. Explain the power of God today.

2. What is He doing today?

3. Explain the Jesus movement in the world today.

WORD OF WISDOM

Show how Jesus' presence is active with us today.

Acts 2:25-28

25 David said about him:

"'I saw the Lord always before me.

Because he is at my right hand,

I will not be shaken.

26 Therefore my heart is glad and my tongue rejoices;

my body also will live in hope,

27 because you will not abandon me to the grave,

nor will you let your Holy one see decay.

28 You have made known to me the paths of life;

you will fill me with joy in your presence.'

The Bible is the truth

The Bible is the truth written down by men who heard the words spoken by the Holy Spirit. Another proof is that He will interpret the validity of them to your heart.

2 Timothy 3:14-17

14 But as for you, continue in what you have learned and have become convinced of, because you know those from whom you learned it, 15 and how from infancy you have known the holy Scriptures, which are able to make you wise for salvation through faith in Christ Jesus. 16 All Scripture is God-breathed and is useful for teaching, rebuking, correcting and training in righteousness, 17 so that the man of God may be thoroughly equipped for every good work.

Jesus said over and over I tell you the truth.

Matthew 5:17-18

17 "Do not think that I have come to abolish the Law or the Prophets; I have not come to abolish them but to fulfill them. 18 I tell you the truth, until heaven and earth disappear, not the smallest letter, not the least stroke of a pen, will by any means disappear from the Law until everything is accomplished.

God watches over His Word to fulfill it.

Isaiah 55:11

11 so is my word that goes out from my mouth:

It will not return to me empty,

but will accomplish what I desire

and achieve the purpose for which I sent it.

David trusted God and proved Him true with his life.

Psalms 25:1-5

To you, O LORD, I lift up my soul;

2 in you I trust, O my God. Do not let me be put to shame, nor let my enemies triumph over me.

3 No one whose hope is in you will ever be put to shame, but they will be put to shame who are treacherous without excuse.

4 Show me your ways, O LORD, teach me your paths;

5 guide me in your truth and teach me, for you are God my Savior, and my hope is in you all day long.

God blessed David, and he became the greatest king.

I read, study, and live the Bible daily the best I can, and it always proves to be true.

I didn't study the Bible and didn't know how to choose a wife. So, I married without consulting the Lord and failed. Next time, when I studied the Bible, I listened to the Lord and married the best one. God was right again.

Now that I read the Bible daily straight through in about a year and a half. The principles and statutes are continually rinsing through my mind so that I am checking and correcting the truth in my heart with the truth in the Bible. I stay open to the Holy Spirit to show me new oracles and ethics to learn and obey. I expectantly look for the teaching of Jesus to correct my spiritual foundation however minute. I love to know and practice Jesus' doctrine exactly.

You cannot make a total teaching out of only one verse in the Bible. It takes the whole Bible to complete a doctrine.

They can get into heresy when they separate an idea away from the context.

I pick titles for books to write that I want to know more about because that makes me study and learn the Bible specifically and practically. I chose this title, 'Hope Beyond Hope,' to learn the relationship between hope and faith and how the power of hope energizes faith.

I need to understand scripture. Plus, I think it is significant enough knowledge that I want other people to know and expand their relationship with God.

In my study, I sensed there was more power in hope than I first thought, and my study proved to be even much more. I now know better how to apply it. This is valuable to me.

Don't stop hoping for the good characteristics of God.

Study the Bible with all your heart, for the best way to live.

Psalms 119:10-14

10 I seek you with all my heart;

do not let me stray from your commands.

11 I have hidden your word in my heart

that I might not sin against you.

12 Praise be to you, O LORD;

teach me your decrees.

13 With my lips I recount

all the laws that come from your mouth.

14 I rejoice in following your statutes

Proverbs 1:7

7 The fear of the LORD is the beginning of knowledge,

POINTS OF INTEREST

1. Do you believe the Bible was written by God?

2. Explain how He watches over His word to perform it.

3. How does it improve the relationship with the Lord when you read it?

WORD OF WISDOM

I have set my heart to know your truth.

Psalms 119:26-30

26 I recounted my ways and you answered me;

teach me your decrees.

27 Let me understand the teaching of your precepts;

then I will meditate on your wonders.

28 My soul is weary with sorrow;

strengthen me according to your word.

29 Keep me from deceitful ways;

be gracious to me through your law.

30 I have chosen the way of truth;

I have set my heart on your laws.

Where do the spiritual qualities reside?

I believe the truth resides between our soul and spirit in my "faith box." I like to think this area is behind the breastbone, near the heart, is my guess. The heart is the epicenter of our living because all the lifeblood goes through there. I know that the brain is control central, and is well able to store and process all the data, but these qualities affect our whole being and through which the work gets done. So, we like to address the heart as our sensitivity target point.

Jesus is the brains of the outfit, but He uses the church people, His body, to do His work. But you might say He does the heavy lifting.

Hebrews 4:12-13

12 For the word of God is living and active. Sharper than any double-edged sword, it penetrates even to dividing soul and spirit, joints and marrow; it judges the thoughts and attitudes of the heart. 13 Nothing in all creation is hidden from God's sight Everything is uncovered and laid bare before the eyes of him to whom we must give account.

This area of our spirit man contains the workings and connection with the Holy Spirit. This section of our anatomy is a busy place where our conscience is taking directions from the Holy Spirit to update our spirit as to the truth of God. Then the conscience runs next door to check on our soul to compare and reconcile the latest revelations. Always be aware that God is watching.

This is the foyer of the room I call the 'faith box' where miracles and truths are kept handy to refer to when you need power for the next prayer and faith request and action.

You can tell that I love to tell this miracle story.

My testimony is that I worked as many Sundays as they asked me. At the end of some months, I became exhausted and had to go to the hospital. In a couple of days, they examined my colon polyp biopsy and found cancer. When the doctor told me I was very nonchalant and said, "Oh I see." No worry or concern about the bad news. My wife, the pastor, and the congregation prayed for me and the doctor removed the polyp and examined it. He came back in two days and told me that I didn't have cancer. My jubilation was laid back because still tired, but happy enough that God healed me in two days. But I still had to spend three weeks recuperating. I calculated that God took back all those Sundays that I worked instead of going to church. I worked that overtime for nothing. That figures, doesn't it?

 In my recollection, I should have caught the warning when this non-Christian asked me how come I worked on Sundays, being a Christian. When I came to my senses I stopped working on Sundays and stopped eating duck food, and white bread, and started eating horse food, oatmeal, and stopped eating only hamburger patties, because you can't get all the grease out of them. These colon polyps are lard collectors and they can get rotten and cause cancer.

After a while, I wondered why I was not bothered by this bad news of cancer. I remembered that two of my friends, Marta Steedman and Lyle Oliver, from church, had been cured of cancer the previous year. My faith box had this power factor handy, so I connected the dots and believed God could heal me too. And He did.

A great source of powerful truths you can refer to and use is the Bible. The miracles in the Bible are in a reference library for your inspection and management to appropriate at the right time. Come into the library of your faith experiences and browse often to recall for future use. It is good to impart them to your children to help them build up their reference library for the future. Remind them to rehearse them to reinforce them to rely on God that helps them and benefits others.

POINTS OF INTEREST

1. What are you putting into your faith box?

2. What power is on hand in your faith box?

3. How do you make this information more useful?

WORD OF WISDOM

Remember the answers to prayer and the miracles to give you a spiritual boost the next time you need them.

Matthew 16:8-12

8 Aware of their discussion, Jesus asked, "You of little faith, why are you talking among yourselves about having no bread? 9 Do you still not understand? Don't you remember the five loaves for the five thousand, and how many basketfuls you gathered? 10 Or the seven loaves for the four thousand, and how many basketfuls you gathered? 11 How is it you don't understand that I was not talking to you about bread? But be on your guard against the yeast of the Pharisees and Sadducees."

Psalms 107:21-22

21 Let them give thanks to the LORD for his unfailing love

and his wonderful deeds for men.

22 Let them sacrifice thank offerings

and tell of his works with songs of joy.

Watch out for the semi-conscience qualities of our DNA

There is another layer below the conscience that tells us what to do. This is the part of our DNA and genes that we inherited from our ancestors and the environment and society we live in by association. We can act and react according to our original nature. Bred into our being are attitudes of who we are that came from our parents and grandparents that form our nature and abilities. Some are wonderful DNA specimens and some are unhelpful. Our DNA can be altered by consistent bad talk or oppression, by negative people and spirits always attacking our better values. We need to go to the Holy Spirit to help us get rid of these negative actions and reactions that are against the truth and righteousness. Other people may be drawn to us and some others may be offended by us, depending on which side of us comes out. Negative or positive words or attitudes are about which situation is happening and who you are with. Our very DNA can be affected and changed by constant contact or abuse. If a person is always confirmed they will be more confident in who they are and what they do, their DNA will change accordingly and it will be passed on to their children. Our inherited genes can be strengthened or diminished to better reign in life through Christ Jesus.

The Lord is good about training us to become Christ-like in every situation. This may take many lessons and tests until we can get it straight. He wants to update and improve our DNA with righteous thinking and actions.

When we find we have some unwholesome words, thoughts, or actions, we need to go to the Holy Spirit and start to root these culprits out of our spirit. A good place to start is prayer, with daily Bible reading and study, regular church attendance, and getting into the presence of Jesus as much as you can. I find praying tongues in the car and at work and home when it can be helpful and refreshing. The Holy Spirit is always available to be with you to talk, sing, or listen, whatever and whenever you want to.

Color your minds with these kinds of thoughts to enhance the fragrance of your presence.

Philippines 4:8

8 Finally, brothers, whatever is true, whatever is noble, whatever is right, whatever is pure, whatever is lovely, whatever is admirable-if anything is excellent or praiseworthy-think about such things.

This a good list to keep in mind to think about thinking about.

- True,
- Noble,
- Right,
- Pure,
- Lovely
- Admirable
- Excellent
- Praiseworthy

Stay away from people's opposite-minded words and thoughts, or they will affect your mind after a while and sway you away from Christ and His righteousness. The Spirits of sinners are strong and persuasive. If you get too much exposure it could change your DNA and slip you out the side door of righteous living. This is true of religion controlling demons and spirits. People who carry them can taint your area and have to be broken off by prayer and rebuking. Put the Bible filter on your TV exposure.

Don't let your mind dwell on these negative, destructive ideas, or they will be hard to shake off.

Colossians 3:5-11

5 Put to death, therefore, whatever belongs to your earthly nature: sexual immorality, impurity, lust, evil desires and greed, which is idolatry. 6 Because of these, the wrath of God is coming.   7 You used to walk in these ways, in the life you once lived. 8 But now you must rid yourselves of all such things as these: anger, rage, malice, slander, and filthy language from your lips. 9 Do not lie to each other, since you have taken off your old self with its practices 10 and have put on the new self, which is being renewed in knowledge in the image of its Creator.

Rude and crude people clash with my spirit and are difficult to witness the Gospel to, even though they need it as much as anybody. It takes a special person or the driving force of the power and boldness of the Holy Spirit to get too chummy with them.

Some people may be called to witness in taverns. I don't think I'm one of them. Although I am most friendly with my workmates, I am still careful not to offend and cut off any following conversation. I like to put out a little 'bait' about Jesus or church to see if they will bite. If there is an open response, I choose a careful tack to expand the conversation. I can use my hobby as an opening, my 'night job' is writing books. Because they are Christian books, I look into their eyes and see what response there is. This gives me an idea of what I can say next. Seldom can I go so far as to lead them to Christ, but make sure that if you can't pick the fruit, don't bruise it. Leave them on a good note,

and hope and pray to add to them another step toward
Christ later. Make every contact a pleasant one.

POINTS OF INTEREST

1. What sways your thinking?
2. How do you stop thinking about negative things?
3. What kind of things do you read?
4. What kind of things do you not read?
5. Do you think that your DNA and character can be changed by bombarding your mind with violence and evil?
6. Can that happen by using mind-altering drugs?

WORD OF WISDOM

Use wisdom in witnessing about your faith.

Ephesians 4:11-16

11 It was he who gave some to be apostles, some to be prophets, some to be evangelists, and some to be pastors and teachers, 12 to prepare God's people for works of service, so that the body of Christ may be built up 13 until we all reach unity in the faith and in the knowledge of the Son of God and become mature, attaining to the whole measure of the fullness of Christ.

14 Then we will no longer be infants, tossed back and forth by the waves, and blown here and there by every wind of teaching and by the cunning and craftiness of men in their deceitful scheming. 15 Instead, speaking the truth in love, we will in all things grow up into him who is the Head, that is, Christ. 16 From him the whole body, joined and held together by every supporting ligament, grows and builds itself up in love, as each part does its work.

Increase in these qualities

In the same way, we increase in these qualities we should increase in faith hope, and trust in the Lord. Do your own Bible study on what God wants for you. It will take you time and effort. Do the best you can to get closer to God.

2 Peter 1:3-9

3 His divine power has given us everything we need for life and godliness through our knowledge of him who called us by his own glory and goodness.

4 Through these he has given us his very great and precious promises, so that through them you may participate in the divine nature and escape the corruption in the world caused by evil desires.

5 For this very reason, make every effort to add to your faith goodness; and to goodness, knowledge;

6 and to knowledge, self-control; and to self-control, perseverance; and to perseverance, godliness;

7 and to godliness, brotherly kindness; and to brotherly kindness, love.

8 For if you possess these qualities in increasing measure, they will keep you from being ineffective and unproductive in your knowledge of our Lord Jesus Christ.

9 But if anyone does not have them, he is nearsighted and blind, and has forgotten that he has been cleansed from his past sins.

Escape the corruption from this world by increasing in:

- **faith**

  Practice having faith and being faithful. Mentally put a precedent on being faithful through your day

so you can recognize it in yourself and others, not to look down on those that aren't, but see where you need to improve. Study the Bible characters for their faithful faith and faithfulness.
Hebrews 11:3-40 some of the people in the Old Testament had faith.

3 By faith we understand that the universe was formed at God's command, so that what is seen was not made out of what was visible.

4 By faith Abel offered God a better sacrifice than Cain did. By faith he was commended as a righteous man, when God spoke well of his offerings. And by faith he still speaks, even though he is dead.

5 By faith Enoch was taken from this life, so that he did not experience death; he could not be found, because God had taken him away. For before he was taken, he was commended as one who pleased God.

6 And without faith it is impossible to please God, because anyone who comes to him must believe that he exists and that he rewards those who earnestly seek him.

7 By faith Noah, when warned about things not yet seen, in holy fear built an ark to save his family. By his faith he condemned the world and became heir of the righteousness that comes by faith.

8 By faith Abraham, when called to go to a place he would later receive as his inheritance, obeyed and went, even though he did not know where he was going. 9 By faith he made his home in the promised land like a stranger in a foreign country; he lived in

tents, as did Isaac and Jacob, who were heirs with him of the same promise. 10 For he was looking forward to the city with foundations, whose architect and builder is God.

11 By faith Abraham, even though he was past age- and Sarah herself was barren-was enabled to become a father because he considered him faithful who had made the promise. 12 And so from this one man, and he as good as dead, came descendants as numerous as the stars in the sky and as countless as the sand on the seashore.

13 All these people were still living by faith when they died. They did not receive the things promised; they only saw them and welcomed them from a distance.

17 By faith Abraham, when God tested him, offered Isaac as a sacrifice. He who had received the promises was about to sacrifice his one and only son, 18 even though God had said to him, "It is through Isaac that your offspring will be reckoned." 19 Abraham reasoned that God could raise the dead, and figuratively speaking, he did receive Isaac back from death.

24 By faith Moses, when he had grown up, refused to be known as the son of Pharaoh's daughter.

29 By faith the people passed through the Red Sea as on dry land; but when the Egyptians tried to do so, they were drowned.

30 By faith the walls of Jericho fell, after the people had marched around them for seven days.

31 By faith the prostitute Rahab, because she welcomed the spies, was not killed with those who were disobedient.

32 And what more shall I say? I do not have time to tell about Gideon, Barak, Samson, Jephthah, David, Samuel and the prophets,

39 These were all commended for their faith, yet none of them received what had been promised. 40 God had planned something better for us so that only together with us would they be made perfect. These were people like us, so we can do it too. Get the faith in your heart like these.

- **goodness**

Where can I do better in being good? Look for ways to be better at goodness. You might be surprised at the atmosphere changes you can make when you come into the room. Be sensitive to others' needs and what you can do to improve the spiritual air. Bring the Lord's joy with you.

- **Knowledge**

Study to show yourself approved not to show off, but in love.

2 Timothy 2:15

15 Study to shew thyself approved unto God, a workman that needeth not to be ashamed, rightly dividing the word of truth KJV

- **self-control**

In society, we need to know and do what is right. We don't want to lead anyone astray, especially the young ones who would look up to us.

1 Peter 5:8-9

8 Be self-controlled and alert. Your enemy the devil prowls around like a roaring lion looking for someone to devour. 9 Resist him, standing firm in the faith, because you know that your brothers throughout the world are undergoing the same kind of sufferings.

Keep a keen eye on how you can respect and reverence God. The world will try to make you think little white lies are OK or do something wrong that everyone else is doing.

- **Perseverance**

This quality needs much strength to proceed because the human tendency is to want to rest and take many breaks. A body gets tired and that's good, but it also wants to relieve that condition ahead of time. When I ran the mile race in track in high school, I never used all my endurance, and only won one race. My coach did not teach me to use all my strength, so I always had some left rather than use it for the race. Now I don't run so much, but I do other tiring things and push myself to finish the project. There are other constraints that call on my attention, so I have to evaluate every action as important as time and timing limits. My wife, at this time, has many things to take care of today, so when I said I would like to take the day off from work, she exuberantly agreed, because she works better when I am at home. It helps her to concentrate on her work. I was happy too because I had a flowing mindset for writing that day. Completion is better than tiredness, but sometimes we get weary and have to deal with that. A nap or coffee helps. I have added Diligence, Determination, and Dedication to this list for it helps me remember to focus on the Discipline of the Lord. There are so many good words and ethics to assist me in perseverance in the ways of the Lord, I have a list to remind me right in my eyes on the wall behind my computer. And four of them start with 'D'. Anything to jog my mind is good.

- **godliness**

Godliness is very near the front of my mind as I try to keep in contact with the Holy Spirit to hear His voice and direction. His presence is valued for His peace and joy, wisdom, knowledge, understanding, and awareness of cautions that I need to pay attention to. Lately, the Holy Spirit has been training me to be more righteous. Like small rules that most people disregard, I am supposed to remember and obey even if they don't. Watch for little things I can do to tidy up the area. I always have a nice attitude toward everybody, even to those who would rather not talk to me. Pray for your leaders and workmates. Do what Jesus would do, even if no one is watching. Don't talk negatively about anybody. Be pleasant, patient, accepting, friendly, and smile. I'm getting new teeth so my smile won't be so distracting. Look at people how Jesus would look at them, and not judge them. Don't do anything that appears ungodly, because

the ungodly know how a Christian should act even
if they Don't do it. Even dirty jokes are too crude.

- **brotherly kindness and love.**

Roman 12:9-21

9 Love must be sincere. Hate what is evil; cling to
what is good. 10 Be devoted to one another in
brotherly love. Honor one another above
yourselves. 11 Never be lacking in zeal, but keep
your spiritual fervor, serving the Lord. 12 Be joyful
in hope, patient in affliction, faithful in prayer. 13
Share with God's people who are in need. Practice
hospitality.

14 Bless those who persecute you; bless and do not
curse. 15 Rejoice with those who rejoice; mourn
with those who mourn. 16 Live in harmony with
one another. Do not be proud, but be willing to
associate with people of low position. Do not be
conceited.

17 Do not repay anyone evil for evil. Be careful to
do what is right in the eyes of everybody. 18 If it is
possible, as far as it depends on you, live at peace
with everyone. 19 Do not take revenge, my friends,
but leave room for God's wrath, for it is written: "It
is mine to avenge; I will repay," says the Lord. 20
On the contrary:

"If your enemy is hungry, feed him;

if he is thirsty, give him something to drink.

In doing this, you will heap burning coals on his
head."

This phrase is difficult to understand in our society.
In the Bible society it means to help someone who

is having a difficult time because that culture had to work hard to start a fire to cook their food or keep warm. And they would carry the hot coals in a container on their head to go home and cook dinner. Then it would do them a favor when they needed it.

21 Do not be overcome by evil, but overcome evil with good.

It is hard to do this whole list. But we try.

Colossians 3:1-10

3:1 Since, then, you have been raised with Christ, set your hearts on things above, where Christ is seated at the right hand of God. 2 Set your minds on things above, not on earthly things. 3 For you died, and your life is now hidden with Christ in God. 4 When Christ, who is your life, appears, then you also will appear with him in glory.

5 Put to death, therefore, whatever belongs to your earthly nature: sexual immorality, impurity, lust, evil desires and greed, which is idolatry. 6 Because of these, the wrath of God is coming.   7 You used to walk in these ways, in the life you once lived. 8 But now you must rid yourselves of all such things as these: anger, rage, malice, slander, and filthy language from your lips. 9 Do not lie to each other, since you have taken off your old self with its practices 10 and have put on the new self, which is being renewed in knowledge in the image of its Creator.

Teach people who will teach people.

2 Timothy 2:1-2

2 And the things you have heard me say in the presence of many witnesses entrust to reliable men who will also be qualified to teach others.

Titus 2:11-15

11 For the grace of God that brings salvation has appeared to all men. 12 It teaches us to say "No" to ungodliness and worldly passions, and to live self-controlled, upright and godly lives in this present age, 13 while we wait for the blessed hope-the glorious appearing of our great God and Savior, Jesus Christ, 14 who gave himself for us to redeem us from all wickedness and to purify for himself a people that are his very own, eager to do what is good.

15 These, then, are the things you should teach. Encourage and rebuke with all authority. Do not let anyone despise you.

Love goes into the area of forgiveness, especially when there is no love lost in the situation and you need to forgive if only to break off the bonds and curses of offenses. Forgiveness puts both parties at rest, both the offender and the offended. This is a spiritual tie that binds freedom to unseen bondage that can hinder progress in other areas as well.

- It is noted that in the **fruit of the Spirit** love is mentioned.

These fruits become evident in your character when you put on Christ and display the likes of Jesus. God is teaching you faith, hope, and trust in Him.

Galatians 5:22-23

22 But the fruit of the Spirit is love, joy, peace, patience, kindness, goodness, faithfulness, 23 gentleness and self-control. Against such things there is no law.

- **love,** When you worship God you start to look like Him in attitude. A person who knows you can sense the change in your disposition in transforming into the image of a loving Jesus.

John 4:7-12

7 Dear friends, let us love one another, for love comes from God. Everyone who loves has been born of God and knows God. 8 Whoever does not love does not know God, because God is love. 9 This is how God showed his love among us: He sent his one and only Son into the world that we might live through him. 10 This is love: not that we loved God, but that he loved us and sent his Son as an atoning sacrifice for our sins. 11 Dear friends, since God so loved us, we also ought to love one another. 12 No one has ever seen God; but if we love one another, God lives in us and his love is made complete in us.

God gives us a tough act to follow, but He will help us complete it.

1 John 4:16

God is love. Whoever lives in love lives in God, and God in him

2 John 5-6

5 And now, dear lady, I am not writing you a new command but one we have had from the beginning. I ask that we love one another. 6 And this is love:

that we walk in obedience to his commands. As you have heard from the beginning, his command is that you walk in love.

The act of unconditional love can alter your DNA so that your life will be changed to the point that your children can inherit the benefits of love and lovely life. Your DNA is not constant but can be changed by strong happenings, whether good or bad. Sometimes you can tell that you have changed after certain inputs. You may be shaped by gaining peace or agitation, by attitudes or persuasions, strong offenses, strong love, or prevalent joy. Your DNA is not always the same but over time is able to be changed by pressure, oppression, or peace and joy, or in a constant loving friendship like marriage. When you get saved, your DNA changes. So, stay connected to Jesus.

I mirror the peaceful, respectful, constantly faithful attitude I was raised in. My Christian grandparents raised me for ten years of my formative life. I generally carry on with their training. My dad and mom divorced when I was about four years old. They had a different atmosphere at home. I know I would have a different character had it not been for my righteous grandparents. In their home, there was not heard a disparaging word.

- **joy,** I enjoy being around people with a joyful peaceful attitude, so I try to carry that mood into each relationship.

- **peace,** Don't react to what is going on around you but respond properly by letting nothing side-track you. Be confident that God is in control, and has your back.

- **patience,** In every circumstance have peace and patience. I'm not in a hurry because God is working out something good for me in this situation.

- **kindness,** The first one we should have kindness for is God. It is imperative for Christians to have the fear of God, which is respect and reverence for Him. We have respect for God by obedience to His Son Jesus so we can be schooled in what to do to be made into the image of Christ. To be reverent to God is to worship Him in body, soul, and spirit to make Him preeminent in our minds as to Who He is and how worthy He is to be worshipped.

- **goodness,** We should express thankfulness for the goodness of God who gave us everything we need.

2 Peter 1:3-4

His divine power has given us everything we need for life and godliness through our knowledge of him who called us by his own glory and goodness. 4 Through these he has given us his very great and precious promises, so that through them you may participate in the divine nature and escape the corruption in the world caused by evil desires.

It is good for us to give to those who have needs we can supply in thankfulness to God.

- **faithfulness,**

You can depend on those who have this fruit. Their integrity is high and honest. My wife said one of the qualities she wanted in a husband was faithfulness. I am honored that I was chosen.

- **gentleness**

  One ad I remember when I was growing up was a strong man holding a piston ring gently with two fingers, "Strong but oh how gentle". This is how a Christian should be in the Kingdom of God.

- **self-control.**

  Be careful to stay away from a bad relationship that could change you into someone you don't want to be, even if it is great for the moment. Always ask the Lord if this is the right way for you to go. Father knows best.

- **increasing measure**

  verse 8 For if you possess these qualities in increasing measure, they will keep you from being ineffective and unproductive in your knowledge of our Lord Jesus Christ.

The amount you have will soon be insufficient. Even though you have love and grace, it is going to wear out and you need a booster shot for the next while, or later that day. Physical energy and the cares of life will take their toll so come back to the Lord for refreshment. Ask the Lord then.

Acts 3:17-20

17 "Now, brothers, I know that you acted in ignorance, as did your leaders. 18 But this is how God fulfilled what he had foretold through all the prophets, saying that his Christ would suffer. 19 Repent, then, and turn to God, so that your sins may be wiped out, that times of refreshing may come from the Lord, 20 and that he may send the Christ, who has been appointed for you-even Jesus.

The increasing of these things requires you to take a break, keep your health up, do things for encouragement, and worship with the saints regularly, I need the presence of the Lord and the people at church. The corporate presence of Jesus helps us spiritually, the physical presence of friends helps us mentally, and the word of God lived and spoken gives us an uplift for our souls to keep all of them fresh and reset.

When I didn't take a break from work, I got tired and sick with cancer. I don't want to increase that.

- 9 **But if anyone does not have them**, he is nearsighted and blind, and has forgotten that he has been cleansed from his past sins.

Be always thought full and thankful for what the Lord has done for you and how He has done it. Your memory should remind you of His goodness and care for you to help you stay on the right track. If you forget His goodness for you, it is easy to slip back into your old ways and can roll back deeper into the swamp than before.

Thank Him often on purpose. In your mind scroll back through His acts of goodness to you when you think of it.

You will most likely have to make a pointed effort to remember God's love for you by pressing into Him and His presence. Life of forgetting His goodness becomes difficult because backsliding is a slippery slope where it gets harder and harder to gain traction to climb back out of the slime. Fortunately, God's love is an open-arms invitation to repent without reprimand for us to come back. He doesn't browbeat you into submission, His way is polite.

Matthew 11:28-30

28 "Come to me, all you who are weary and burdened, and I will give you rest. 29 Take my yoke upon you and learn from me, for I am gentle and humble in heart, and you will

find rest for your souls. 30 For my yoke is easy and my burden is light."

Repeat this as many times as you need rest and peace.

I know a divorced lady missionary who was asked to be another missionary's wife, but she wouldn't. I think she had more wisdom and asked the Lord which way to go. She had gotten into a couple of messes before, so caution before the Lord was prudent.

Study to show yourself approved and wise to choose God's way as soon as you can.

2 Timothy 2:15

15 Do your best to present yourself to God as one approved, a workman who does not need to be ashamed and who correctly handles the word of truth.

The answers are in the Bible, now it is up to us to find them and remember them. Rehearse them as often as you can.

POINTS OF INTEREST

1. Should we add more attributes of God to this list?

2. How would you make these items stronger?

3. How do you remember these things?

4. How do you add to your faith?

5. What grade would you give yourself on these lists?

WORD OF WISDOM

Hebrews 5:11-6:3

1 We have much to say about this, but it is hard to explain because you are slow to learn. 12 In fact, though by this time you ought to be teachers, you need someone to teach you the elementary truths of God's word all over again. You need milk, not solid food! 13 Anyone who lives on milk, being still an infant, is not acquainted with the teaching about righteousness. 14 But solid food is for the mature, who by constant use have trained themselves to distinguish good from evil.

Hebrews 6

6:1 Therefore let us leave the elementary teachings about Christ and go on to maturity, not laying again the foundation of repentance from acts that lead to death, and of faith in God, 2 instruction about baptisms, the laying on of hands, the resurrection of the dead, and eternal judgment. 3 And God permitting, we will do so.

Learn the dynamics of the Spirit

The Holy Spirit is God's Spirit and is the third person of the trinity and He works in the same mind as the Father and Jesus. He is the One whom Jesus sent back to Earth when He ascended to Heaven to sit on the right side of the Father. By the hand of the Holy Spirit, a God movement was started 2000 years ago and has increased unstoppable in building the Kingdom of God on earth.

Ephesians 4:7-13

7 But to each one of us grace has been given as Christ apportioned it. 8 This is why it says:

"When he ascended on high,

he led captives in his train

and gave gifts to men."

9 (What does "he ascended" mean except that he also descended to the lower, earthly regions? 10 He who descended is the very one who ascended higher than all the heavens, in order to fill the whole universe.) 11 It was he who gave some to be apostles, some to be prophets, some to be evangelists, and some to be pastors and teachers, 12 to prepare God's people for works of service, so that the body of Christ may be built up 13 until we all reach unity in the faith and in the knowledge of the Son of God and become mature, attaining to the whole measure of the fullness of Christ.

These ministries are provided by Christ to prepare God's people for works of service, so that the body of Christ may be built up. These offices are to train others.

- apostles
- prophets,
- evangelists,
- pastors
- teachers,

This Holy Spirit also covers the world to work in all people to draw them to Christ. His mind is all-knowing from the beginning to forever in Eternity. He knows every glitch in mankind, why it came, and where it is going. The Godhead has it all mapped out for each one and scripture will be fulfilled.

Isaiah is alluding to a new Heaven and new earth but only hints at the timeline.

Isaiah 65:17

17 "Behold, I will create new heavens and a new earth. The former things will not be remembered, nor will they come to mind.

Jesus leaves room for a time expenditure when different people die and go to Heaven.

John 14:1-3

14:1 Let not your heart be troubled: ye believe in God, believe also in me.

2 In my Father's house are many mansions: if it were not so, I would have told you. I go to prepare a place for you.

3 And if I go and prepare a place for you, I will come again, and receive you unto myself; that where I am, there ye may be also.

In the meanwhile, we are to be doing His bidding in obedience to building the Kingdom of God on Earth. We do this by occupying as an overcoming army. We are to be busy building the Kingdom of God on earth. With all the technological improvement I can see maybe one hundred years yet to go.

Luke 19:12-13

12 He said therefore, A certain nobleman went into a far country to receive for himself a kingdom, and to return.

13 And he called his ten servants, and delivered them ten pounds, and said unto them, Occupy till I come. KJV

Peter is preparing us to finally leave earth but to do Jesus' work until then.

What kind of people should we be?

2 Peter 3:11-13

11 Since everything will be destroyed in this way, what kind of people ought you to be? You ought to live holy and godly lives 12 as you look forward to the day of God and speed its coming. That day will bring about the destruction of the heavens by fire, and the elements will melt in the heat. 13 But in keeping with his promise we are looking forward to a new heaven and a new earth, the home of righteousness.

I believe that Revelation is the end result of the whole Kingdom of Heaven complete after God does away with this dirtball earth.

A missiologist calculated there are half the unreached people in the world about 3 billion people in South East Asia. So, we have a big job before us.

We are called to take the gospel to the world.

Matthew 24:14

14 And this gospel of the kingdom shall be preached in all the world for a witness unto all nations; and then shall the end come. KJV

God is concerned about each of His children He made uniquely with tender, loving, care.

 Matthew 18:14

14 Even so it is not the will of your Father which is in heaven, that one of these little ones should perish. KJV

Romans 11:25

25 I do not want you to be ignorant of this mystery, brothers, so that you may not be conceited: Israel has experienced a hardening in part until the full number of the Gentiles has come in.

God wants a representative from every tribe language, people, and nation, as representatives of the Kingdom of God on this earth before the end.

Revelation 5:9-10

9 And they sang a new song:

"You are worthy to take the scroll

and to open its seals,

because you were slain,

and with your blood you purchased men for God

from every tribe and language and people and nation.

10 You have made them to be a kingdom and priests to serve our God,

and they will reign on the earth."

Then Heaven will be the final resting place that will be glorious beyond measure or imagination for all God's people.

Revelation 21:1-5

21:1 Then I saw a new heaven and a new earth, for the first heaven and the first earth had passed away, and there was no longer any sea. 2 I saw the Holy City, the new Jerusalem, coming down out of heaven from God, prepared as a bride beautifully dressed for her husband. 3 And I heard a loud voice from the throne saying, "Now the dwelling of God is with men, and he will live with them. They will be his people, and God himself will be with them and be their God. 4 He will wipe every tear from their eyes. There will be no more death or mourning or crying or pain, for the old order of things has passed away."

5 He who was seated on the throne said, "I am making everything new!" Then he said, "Write this down, for these words are trustworthy and true."

POINTS OF INTEREST

1. In Eternity, Heaven is being prepared and will be ready for each of us to arrive. What do you think is the timing of these events?

2. What do you think Heaven will look like?

3. Explain the new Heavens and the new earth.

4. Explain the dynamics of Jesus being our Faith, Hope, and our trust.

5. How do we speed up the second coming of Jesus?

WORD OF WISDOM

The Spirit helps us to be faithful and steadfast.

Ephesians 4:14-16

14 Then we will no longer be infants, tossed back and forth by the waves, and blown here and there by every wind of teaching and by the cunning and craftiness of men in their deceitful scheming. 15 Instead, speaking the truth in love, we will in all things grow up into him who is the Head, that is, Christ. 16 From him the whole body, joined and held together by every supporting ligament, grows and builds itself up in love, as each part does its work.

The Holy Spirit helps us in all things love.

1 Peter 4:7-11

7 The end of all things is near. Therefore be clear minded and self-controlled so that you can pray. 8 Above all, love each other deeply, because love covers over a multitude of sins. 9 Offer hospitality to one another without grumbling. 10 Each one should use whatever gift he has received to serve others, faithfully administering God's grace in its various forms. 11 If anyone speaks, he should do it as one speaking the very words of God. If anyone serves, he should do it with the strength God provides, so that in all things God may be praised through Jesus Christ. To him be the glory and the power for ever and ever. Amen.

Break off what hinders

Strength comes by keeping connected to Jesus to the end.

Hebrews 12:1-3

12:1 Therefore, since we are surrounded by such a great cloud of witnesses, let us throw off everything that hinders and the sin that so easily entangles, and let us run with perseverance the race marked out for us. 2 Let us fix our eyes on Jesus, the author and perfecter of our faith, who for the joy set before him endured the cross, scorning its shame, and sat down at the right hand of the throne of God. 3 Consider him who endured such opposition from sinful men, so that you will not grow weary and lose heart.

Every day we run into things that could hinder us. There are numerous things that can hinder the love of money is a big item because therein is power and ability. Do not choose mammon.

Luke 16:13

13 No servant can serve two masters: for either he will hate the one, and love the other; or else he will hold to the one, and despise the other. Ye cannot serve God and mammon. KJV

Solomon had greed problems.

2 Chronicles 9:13-14

13 The weight of the gold that Solomon received yearly was 666 talents, 14 not including the revenues brought in by merchants and traders.

I think the 'the beast' is money worship.

Revelation 13:16-18

16 He also forced everyone, small and great, rich and poor, free and slave, to receive a mark on his right hand or on his forehead, 17 so that no one could buy or sell unless he had the mark, which is the name of the beast or the number of his name.

18 This calls for wisdom. If anyone has insight, let him calculate the number of the beast, for it is man's number. His number is 666.

Colossians 3:5-10

5 Put to death, therefore, whatever belongs to your earthly nature: sexual immorality, impurity, lust, evil desires and greed, which is idolatry. 6 Because of these, the wrath of God is coming. 7 You used to walk in these ways, in the life you once lived. 8 But now you must rid yourselves of all such things as these: anger, rage, malice, slander, and filthy language from your lips. 9 Do not lie to each other, since you have taken off your old self with its practices 10 and have put on the new self, which is being renewed in knowledge in the image of its Creator.

Repentance is the order of the day.

John the Baptist started preaching.

Matthew 3:2

2 and saying, "Repent, for the kingdom of heaven is near.

Jesus started preaching.

Matthew 4:17

17 From that time on Jesus began to preach, "Repent, for the kingdom of heaven is near."

Peter started preaching the same thing.

Acts 2:38-39

38 Peter replied, "Repent and be baptized, every one of you, in the name of Jesus Christ for the forgiveness of your sins. And you will receive the gift of the Holy Spirit.

Repentance breaks the circle of death.

God is serious about repenting which is to stop sinning and do what God wants you to do.

Then you are free to obey Jesus and enter life with Jesus and break off the curse of death.

Matthew 19:17

17 "Why do you ask me about what is good?" Jesus replied. "There is only one who is good. If you want to enter life, obey the commandments."

1 John 1:1-2

1:1 That which was from the beginning, which we have heard, which we have seen with our eyes, which we have looked at and our hands have touched-this we proclaim concerning the Word of life. 2 The life appeared; we have seen it and testify to it, and we proclaim to you the eternal life, which was with the Father and has appeared to us.

Philippians 2:13-16

13 For it is God which worketh in you both to will and to do of his good pleasure.

14 Do all things without murmurings and disputings:

15 That ye may be blameless and harmless, the sons of God, without rebuke, in the midst of a crooked and perverse nation, among whom ye shine as lights in the world;

16 Holding forth the word of life; that I may rejoice in the day of Christ, that I have not run in vain, neither laboured in vain. KJV

POINTS OF INTEREST

1. Do you think that 666 is a problem?
2. What does 666 represent?
3. Why is repentance so important?
4. How do you repent?

WORD OF WISDOM

The Bible shows you how to get out of this mess.

Acts 3:17-20

17 "Now, brothers, I know that you acted in ignorance, as did your leaders. 18 But this is how God fulfilled what he had foretold through all the prophets, saying that his Christ would suffer. 19 Repent, then, and turn to God, so that your sins may be wiped out, that times of refreshing may come from the Lord, 20 and that he may send the Christ, who has been appointed for you-even Jesus.

Do not lose hope. The Holy Spirit will help you.